WHAT THEY *DON'T* TEACH YOU AT HOTEL SCHOOLS

Notes from 4 Continents

Jan Kirstein

Contents

FOREWORD

The bestseller, *What They Don't Teach You at Harvard Business School* is my inspiration for this book.

Between the theories of business school and the real world of business, there is a gap that can only be filled by real-life experiences. This is the premise behind the referenced book, which was published in 1984 and written by Marc H. McCormack, one of the most successful entrepreneurs in American business. With a handshake with the golfer Arnold Palmer and less than a thousand dollars, he started International Management Group (IMG) and, over a four-decade period, built the company into a multimillion-dollar enterprise with offices in more than thirty countries.

What They Don't Teach You at Hotel Schools follows the idea of McCormack's book, i.e., certain aspects of business must be experienced and cannot be taught in the school environment.

With more than 40 years' experience in the hotel industry, I take the risk and challenge with the title, despite not having attended a hotel school. I hope to contribute to the knowledge and awareness of future hoteliers. An educated guess is that many successful hoteliers have a hotel school background, which has given them a base for their future in the industry. The idea of this book is to complement the theory, and the relatively limited practice, that a hotel school education can provide, with real-life anecdotes – examples of what to look out for and to provide some "food for thought". This also applies to non-hotel school academics who aim to join the hotel industry. There are probably as many successful hoteliers who have chosen not to enroll in a hotel school.

In addition to my own thoughts and conclusions, some friends and former colleagues have been kind enough to contribute with their wisdom and insights.

Dear reader, if your goal is to entertain the hotel profession in your hometown with a nice independent hotel, you might not find a lot of "meat on the bones." However, more to eat for those of you who are considering a career with an international hotel company. Maybe even the seasoned hotelier will find a few "eye-openers." The book is centered around the issues and challenges of the General Manager. A slice of asset management is also covered.

Never worry about age and retirement, it's a fantastic freedom which, amongst others, can give you time to write a book. No doubt there is a big number of far more experienced and successful hoteliers, and former hoteliers, than the author. However, this one has had enough free time, in old age, to jot down on paper an interesting part of life.

(A BIT OF) MY JOURNEY

Europe – North Africa – Middle East – Southeast Asia – Europe – Asia and Australia – Europe - that's my journey.

Born in 1954, raised, with a happy childhood, in a suburb of Stockholm, Sweden – sports, sports and sports with my three year older brother and friends. High School in my hometown, Lidingö, language studies in France, military service, bachelor's degree in economics, University of Stockholm. Waiter and real estate sales in Florida, USA, substitute teacher, sales at a sports marketing company, admin job in the insurance industry – At this point, I had enough of non-engaging jobs and wrote a letter to the Director of Human Resources at Sheraton Stockholm Hotel. I have never regretted this letter as it kicked off my life in the hotel industry. My journey started as Sales Executive at Sheraton

Stockholm Hotel in 1982, at the age of 27 and, as an employee, ended 2020 in Bangkok as VP Asset Management with Gaw Capital Partners Hospitality (GCPH).

Since then, I have entertained some freelance assignments in Scandinavia.

A few milestones:

– 1984, the first pre-opening experience, as Director of Sales of Sheraton Hotel Oslo Fjord, Norway.

– 1988, the first assignment outside Scandinavia, as Executive Assistant Manager of Sheraton Limassol, Cyprus.

– 1994, a special experience, as Resident Manager, in charge of the closing of Sheraton Istanbul, Turkey.

– February 1994, Victor our first born.

– 1995, my first position as General Manager (GM), Sheraton Hammamet, Tunisia

– August 1996, Our second child, Emilie.

– 2002, the first experience in the Middle East, GM of Sheraton Amman Al Nabil Hotel & Towers, Jordan.

– 2006, time for Southeast Asia, as GM of

Sheraton Grande Laguna Phuket, A Luxury Collection Resort, Thailand.

– 2011, GM of a “Monster”, the 1072 room Regal Airport Hotel, Hong Kong.

– 2015, “the dark side,” i.e., representing hotel investors as VP Asset Management at GCPH in Bangkok, Thailand.

All positions and locations in appendix 1.

There are obvious challenges when moving from destination to destination, but more importantly, it gives you a great adrenaline kick. It’s an opportunity to experience something totally new, professionally, and privately, to make an impact in a new business environment, to start from scratch and go full speed—fantastic!

“The world is a book, and those who do not travel read only one page.” —Saint Augustine.

WHY BECOME A HOTELIER

Hotelier - I think it's in your blood, in your backbone, in your DNA - call it whatever!

I remember when I, a bit nervous, entered the office of Mr. Jan Ling of Wretman Restaurants in Stockholm. The office was located on top of Restaurant Riche, one of the many famous establishments of the Wretman group of restaurants. Mr. Ling was a partner of the legendary restaurateur Tore Wretman. More importantly for me, he was the Swedish representative for the hotel and restaurant faculty of Cornell University in Ithaca, New York. I did not have any experience in the hotel industry, and I do not remember from where, but I had heard that Cornell University represented the best hotel education there was. At the age of 21, I was determined to become a hotelier with a world-class education as the base. I have to say that I was very naïve, for two reasons. Firstly, I did not consider the expense of my eventual studies at Cornell. Secondly, and this suddenly hit me hard, I realized that my command of the English language was not good enough. I was not able to complete the application form to Cornell as I couldn't fully comprehend all the questions. Embarrassed I left the office of Mr. Ling with an unfinished application form, realizing that this eventual adventure had to be postponed. "It's in your blood"—I was still determined to one day join the hotel industry.

What is the attraction of the hotel industry?

Hotels are a bit of a mystery when you do not know the business. What's going on in that building? People sleep and eat there, but what else? There is also the misperception of glamour. It's such a multi-faceted working environment. The mix of guests and cultures, the pace, check-ins/check-outs, the bar, the restaurants, smiles and tears, the business traveler, the leisure guest, conferences, exhibitions, shops, weddings, functions, parties. All the "non-visible" like kitchens, engineering, planning, staffing, finance, sales, marketing.

The further you climb in the hierarchy of a hotel, the more exposed you are to the beauty of the "hotel village". I cannot imagine a better, more exciting, business environment than a vibrant and busy hotel. The hotelier choosing to join one of the major international hotel companies can also add the thrill of experiencing different cultures, with its beauty and challenges, and the joy of building a social network of friends around the world. Just be prepared that the hotel business never takes a break; it is as important on a weekend as on a weekday, at 03.00 am as at 03.00 pm, on Christmas Eve as on any other day, it is 24/7, 52 weeks a year.

The most important and never to forget: The constant pressure to produce sufficient returns to the financial stakeholders.

Let me quote a former Resident Manager with whom I once worked, now an experienced GM:

> "Dear future hotelier,
>
> It's not a flashy business; it involves hard work, numerous extra hours (unpaid, of course), dealing with demanding guests and owners—some great, some, well, better left without comment. They are high or low maintenance, however, you develop lifelong friendships with some. The same holds true for peers and colleagues. To add to the challenge, there's an owner representative and a head office overseeing your every

move. Your responsibilities include reports, dashboards, tasks, instructions, ticking boxes, completing various assignments, record-keeping, audits, and more. And let's not forget, there's always someone who claims to know your job better than you, offering advice on how to do things. Keep smiling, express gratitude, but stay true to yourself. As a hotelier, you play multiple roles—a confidant, leader, follower, doctor, lawyer, compliance officer, salesperson, waiter, cook, priest, rabbi, sheikh, engineer, bookkeeper, plotter, doer, psychologist, housekeeper, wellness guru—essentially, a jack of all trades, perhaps a master of one or two."

There are two sides to the coin!

CULTURAL DIFFERENCES

Sensitivity

Based on my experience, and the comments of many colleagues, international hotel companies are not doing a good enough job in preparing their GMs, and other key people, for the challenges that they will face when taking up an assignment in a new, and often unknown, destination. You are being "thrown into the deep end of the pool," sometimes on a short notice. There are many things to consider—religion, language, habits, taboos, perception of expatriates, i.e. yourself, to name a few evident ones. Hotel companies will hopefully improve in support of international relocations. In the meantime, as much own homework as possible is the obvious recipe.

Despite, or maybe thanks to, minimum

onboarding, usually a few days hand-over with the respective predecessor, my transitions to new destinations went all very smoothly, and I adapted fast to new environments.

There was one embarrassing incident, that can be considered as "the exception to the rule" and can serve as a good lesson.

"Good morning girls!" This was the way one morning, in the year 2001, I kicked off the morning meeting in Soma Bay, a stunning Sheraton resort on the Red Sea in Egypt. Nothing wrong with the greeting, however, except that for Franz, our Executive Assistant Manager from Austria and Helga, our German Executive Housekeeper, the meeting participants were all Egyptian men. In this environment, a more insulting greeting is hard to find. I did catch bad vibes, however "Mr. Funny", as I thought I was, used the same greeting the following morning. I knew it wasn't appropriate, however after close to two years as their GM, I thought my relation to this group of colleagues was of such strong nature, that I could get away with the stupid, non-sensitive, morning greeting. Why even push my luck? I did NOT get away with it!

Twice was two times too many, and two of the department heads decided to address the issue to the top man of the Red Sea Tourist Police, by writing an anonymous letter of complaint. I got "my fingers slapped" by the gentleman in question in a short and not very friendly meeting in his office. I had to stand up during the meeting, I did not deserve to sit down as I had insulted his countrymen. The Tourist Police also paid a visit to my boss in Cairo, stressing the discontent with the GM of Sheraton Soma Bay.

My morning greeting represents an obvious lack of sensitivity. Writing an anonymous letter to the authorities represents a culture where you prefer not to confront authority face-to-face, you rather do it in a non-direct manner. Authority plays a much bigger role in the Middle East and in Asia compared to Europe. This is of great importance when you are on top of the hierarchy, even as a GM of a hotel. You are the Big Boss, and you are the role model, never to forget. Another important issue in the Middle East, and even more so in Asia, is that you should never put a subordinate, or anyone, in a situation that could put the person at risk of "losing face," e.g., no criticism in front of others, though fine behind closed doors.

One famous quote by American civil rights activist and author Maya Angelou goes: "I've learned that people will forget what you said, people will forget what you did, but people will never forget how you made them feel." (The Guardian) "First-time travelers in Asia often end up perplexed after witnessing some inexplicable, what-just-happened scenarios. For instance, sometimes, letting someone be wrong is just better than *pointing out* they are wrong. Causing someone public embarrassment in any form is an unforgivable no-no." (Trip Savvy)

I did figure out who wrote the famous letter, however I dealt with it my way and never confronted the authors, maybe I was afraid of losing face.

Corruption

"The abuse of entrusted power for private gain," is a simple definition of corruption. (Transparency International)

Transparency International is a global movement working in over 100 countries to end the injustice of corruption. Every year this organization publishes a CPI, Corruption Perceptions Index, that ranks 180 countries and territories around the world by their perceived levels of public sector corruption.

The results are given on a scale of 0 (highly corrupt) to 100 (very clean).

In 2023, like in 2022, the global average was just 43 out of a possible 100 points.

More than two-thirds of countries score below 50, indicating that they have serious corruption problems.

A few examples from the published CPI of 2023; 1. Denmark (90), 5. Singapore (83), 14. Australia (75), 20. United Kingdom (71), 20. France (71), 24. USA (69), 26. UAE (68) 42. Italy (56), 63. Jordan (46), 76. China (42), 83. South Africa (41), 87. Tunisia (40), 87. Colombia (40), 98. Argentina (37), 104. Ukraine (36), 108. Thailand (35), 108. Egypt (35), 115. Turkey (34), 141. Russia (26), 145. Nigeria (25), 180. Somalia (11). (Transparency International)

Right or wrong, my assumption is basic - if the public sector is corrupt, so is the private sector. I have worked in several countries with low CPI, i.e., countries with relatively high level of corruption, as per Transparency International: Jordan, Malaysia, Tunisia, Turkey, Thailand and Egypt, all with a CPI below 50. As a Swede (CPI 82), it takes a bit of adaptation. My approach was always the same, i.e., I cannot change society, however I can do my very best to establish a "clean working environment."

Easier said than done!

In 1995, I got my first assignment as General Manager with the ITT Sheraton organization. I made the important step from number two to number one. My dream came true 13 years after I got my first Sheraton business card as Sales Executive at the Sheraton Stockholm Hotel. I proudly went to Tunisia as GM of the Sheraton Hammamet Resort. As a hotelier, I was well prepared after being second in command for a total of six and a half years in Limassol, Antalya, Algarve, and Istanbul.

In Hammamet, I realized that I oversaw a hotel that had some key people contributing to the low CPI of Tunisia. I put down my foot, and not too long after I arrived, fired the Purchasing Manager—"strike one." This created "some healthy tension" amongst the department heads. I now had my eyes on the next key person, let this person be named "Alie." Only strong suspicions, nothing solid, until year two when we were planning a major renovation of the resort. The renovation of all guest rooms, public areas, and the restaurants could have secured a healthy amount of money for me, as I was approached by several potential suppliers to improve my private balance sheet. The "front" and coordinator for the renovation was Alie. This person had all the established contacts with contractors and suppliers and was the key to a successful renovation. I was convinced that without Alie, I would not be able to finalize the renovation on time and within budget. The Sheraton Hammamet was 50% owned by the ITT Sheraton Corporation, the only hotel in Africa and the Middle East, and one of the very few hotels worldwide with equity, hence a bit of extra attention, and pressure, from the corporate office.

I became quite close to the artist who produced the artwork for the renovation, and he presented a copy of a check issued to Alie. To me, this was solid evidence on hand, and I was prematurely celebrating "strike two." The artist was not willing to hand me a copy of the check as this could then be wrongly taken as proof of a bribe on his part. This was not the case, I had decided on the artwork, but Alie still received a check from the artist. In this environment, the artist had no choice, and he was not surprised or upset. It was the way business was conducted, no big deal.

I needed Alie for the renovation, still knowing he was "on the take." It was all completed timely within budget, and it was truly a nice upgrade of the resort. The corrupt system beat me, I accepted it and there was never a "strike two". For me, the obvious question is, could I have let go of Alie, even though I was not in the position to present firm evidence, and still succeed with the renovation? It would have been a risky undertaking, and I will never know what eventual "revenge actions" Alie would have taken if fired. My highest priority was to carry out the renovation as per plan, whatever it took. First-time GM and not being able to handle a renovation - no way Jose'! It was a bit like being "between a rock and a hard place." No Alie, and potentially not a successful renovation, in addition to lost business and lost credibility on my part. Alie, and a close to guaranteed success of the project, however always knowing that I had given in to a way of conducting business that is contradicting to my moral compass. I do not regret the way I dealt with the situation though to this day, I am not convinced that I took the correct route.

This story highlights the difficulties that you can face when operating in a non-familiar environment. It could be an interesting subject for discussion in any hotel school. It also strongly relates to another section in the book, *Work Ethics.*

After 4 ½ years in Tunisia, it was time for Egypt and the Red Sea. At this moment in time, 1999, we were a family of four, with Victor 5 years old and Emilie 3 years old. The container with family belongings was filled up, to be shipped to the new site of adventure. No container leaves the country before it's been approved by the finance authorities, a standard procedure to make sure that the sender has paid all taxes relating to the tenure in Tunisia. My taxes were paid by the hotel, and I was, to say the least, surprised to be contacted by a representative of the finance department claiming that I had not fulfilled my tax obligations. This had to be settled before our container could leave for Egypt. The authorities claimed that I had to pay taxes on my benefits, mainly housing, car and food and beverage. As per our auditors, that we used as advisers, this is not what the tax law prescribes. I was advised that we would easily win an eventual court case. In 4 ½ years, the claimed amount had accumulated to be sizeable and would not be healthy for the finances of this relatively small resort. The claim to pay additional taxes was disputed and the family left for Egypt with a container stuck in the port of Tunis.

Prior to leaving, Hedi, our Director of Finance, and I had discussions about paying the right person the right amount of money to release the container. This was rejected by all parties involved, including the Sheraton corporate HR department, not surprisingly. The discussions with the authorities dragged on and we finally, one year later (!), after having paid the right person the right amount of money, received our stuff in Egypt. Nice to finally welcome the kids' toys, bicycles, PC etc. I regret not having paid from the start, as in the end, it became a question of paying anyway. I had stretched my patience to the absolute limit to be a "good citizen." Even if we would have succeeded the legal way, I am convinced that it would have become a very long legal battle and we would have had to redirect the container to Jordan, or even Thailand, our destinations following the 2 1/2 years in Egypt.

I have encountered corruption and bribes, in various forms, on many occasions, and I do not have the answer to how to deal with it. It's recommended to play safe, cover your rear, and ask for written advice from your corporate office or owner. This is the most decent suggestion, even if it might not always lead to a desirable outcome.

Languages

The best way to show that you embrace a new culture is to learn the language, or at least, to a minimum, make sure to pick up more than just the most common greeting phrases. Don't be afraid, just go for it. With one exception, French in Tunisia, I'm embarrassed to say that I personally failed miserably.

It's interesting the way certain words and expressions are used in different cultures. In Thailand, I had a couple of fascinating experiences. At the Sheraton in Phuket, when on my "morning round," a young girl behind the front desk greeted me: "Morning Boss, you look very sexy today!" Wow, hardly what you would hear in Jordan, my previous environment in the Middle East. This was not a sign of disrespect, on the contrary, just a way to give a compliment in a culture where the word "sexy" is used more liberally than in most other cultures. I also learned an expression in Thailand, totally non-related to hotels, though worthwhile to mention. This played out in Bangkok, a Sunday round of golf at the beautiful Thai Country Club, operated by the Peninsula Hotels. My female caddie was a bit slow and looked exhausted already after nine holes, why I asked her if she was OK. She looked at me with tired eyes and said in a sleepy voice: "Boss, too much sexercise last night." Sexercise, I'd never heard that one before.

Expectations and Perceptions vs. Reality

There are always surprises, positive and negative, when you experience a new destination and an unknown culture. You will obviously be biased towards the people and culture that are going to be the essence of your new life. The perception remains reality until you are proven wrong.

The whole little family arrived in Phuket in December 2005. In addition to the 410 hotel rooms, Sheraton also managed several nice villas situated around the nearby Laguna golf course, and one of these villas had been allocated for us. We arrived in the late evening and were welcomed by a row of beautifully dressed Thai women dancing and throwing flower petals on us, accompanied by candles and soft Thai music. Indoors, we were greeted by all department heads. The kids were overwhelmed by the welcome and immediately went for cover in a bedroom. Tasty Thai food and drinks - What a fantastic way to start a new life in Southeast Asia. You expect to have a nice welcome as the new General Manager, however this was certainly a "cultural shock" – a beautiful memory.

Travel to Thailand, and you will experience the best available service in the hotel industry worldwide. This was my idea of the level of service in Thailand, before having set my foot in this beautiful country. I was convinced that our welcome to Phuket just highlighted the true Thai service culture – “The Land of Smiles”.

Unfortunately, I was wrong. Overall, more than acceptable service, but still not up to my very high expectations. It really surprised me, and it was a disappointment. Phuket is the “tourist mecca” of Thailand and had over the years been spoiled by relatively full hotels, which resulted in nice amounts of service charge distributed to the staff at the end of the month, regardless of service level. Many employees in the hotel industry had become spoiled. Harsh words, maybe I had put the bar too high as a reflection of nice destination articles and professional ads and commercials.

Based on an assignment many years later, as Area GM of Minor Hotels’ owned Anantara properties from Chang Rai in the north to Phuket in the south, I agree with the statement that service in general improves the further north in Thailand you travel. There are obviously exceptions, and you can find resorts in Phuket being world renowned for exceptional service.

For whatever reason, I did not associate

Thailand with labor unions. This should be a Swedish specialty. The second misperception. At the Sheraton Phuket, we had a relatively small group that represented the unionized staff members. To me, their prime objective seemed to be to battle the management, regardless of the topic, even if it would be something positive and advantageous for the associates of the hotel. This was best exemplified when we, the management, prior to announcing to all staff members, called for a meeting with the union representatives to communicate the great news that the hotel was transiting from a 6-day working week to a 5-day working week, keeping the same salaries. It's not often you can deliver this kind of news. Work 17% fewer hours with the same pay. When the boss of the union started to argue against (!) a 5-day working week, I did what I have only done twice in my professional life— I left the meeting room. The 5-day working week was soon thereafter successfully implemented.

Arriving in Langkawi in December 2010, I did not know what to expect in "any shape or form" as I had not done my homework and I did not know anyone to contact who had an experience of working in Malaysia. Here I found the best level of service that I have ever encountered. By service, I mean true friendliness and hospitality with a smile and, most importantly, genuine concern for the wellbeing of the guests. With no disrespect to the Malaysian associates, who were great, the recipe for the outstanding level of service was the employees from the Philippines. What a fantastic feeling to walk around in the resort as GM and never (!) be concerned that the guests are not being treated like royalty. Occasionally, the cutlery was placed wrongly when setting up a table for service, who cares?

Back to Thailand, "expect the unexpected." In Thailand, nothing should be unexpected. During my close to eleven years in Thailand, 2006 – 2020 with a few "detours," I experienced two military coups, violent street fights between different political sympathizers ("red and yellow shirts"), demonstrators closing Bangkok airport, strike in Phuket, and bomb detonating in central Bangkok. We had SARS, bird flu and financial meltdown—nothing stops the Thai society from a fast recovery and to start all over. The Thai people must have something in their culture allowing them to refrain from the negative of the past and solely focus on a more positive future, truly amazing.

Many years earlier, after a combined seven years

in Arab countries, Tunisia and Egypt, I felt comfortable with the move to Jordan in 2002. However it was a massive difference between working in a business hotel and living in a capital city, compared to the resort environment. What I had not experienced, before arriving in Jordan, was the use of personal connections, "wasta" in Arabic, which is a common practice and a social norm in many Arab countries. "A friend of a friend" who has a son or daughter who would like to join the hotel industry. It happened countless times and quite often my "diplomatic skills" were put to the test. Especially when Mr. Nadim Mouasher, a true gentleman and chairman of the owning company had a request from the Royal Court. A youngster, with no previous experience of working in hotels, was interested in starting at the Sheraton, ideally at department head level. The absolute minimum I could do was to arrange an interview with the young man. As Mr. Nadim also controlled and was the chairman of the Marriott hotel in Amman, I thereafter suggested the Marriott to be more suitable. Mr. Nadim did not push the issue, and I was off the hook.

Four of my department heads at the Sheraton Grande Laguna in Phuket were Aussies. What characterized them was that they were professional, reliable, and hard workers with a good sense of humor. As a General Manager, one cannot ask for more from the closest co-workers. Seven years after I had left Sheraton Phuket in 2010, I visited Perth in Australia several times. We, Gaw Capital Partners Hospitality, had an interesting project to convert an office building into part student accommodation and part hostel. A local company was engaged as project manager, and I thought I would meet up with the same kind of approach to work as I experienced from my ex-colleagues in Phuket. To be fair, they did their job, but not at the pace that I was accustomed to. I used to say that if you work with Aussies in Perth, their working hours are short and their lunch break is long, as they should not only eat, but they also need time to wax their surfboards. Once again, perception is reality until you are proven wrong.

Even within Europe, one does not have to travel far to experience big cultural differences. A strong memory is my short stint in Munich. Awaiting my transfer to Tunisia, I spent one month, in December of 1994, at the Sheraton Munich Hotel to support with the handover of the hotel to the new owning company. To be perfectly honest, it was a hotel that could pick up my salary whilst I was getting ready for the next move. The context was that my previous experience in closing the Sheraton Istanbul would be beneficial – maybe it was.

The Germans have never been accused of being too laid back; on the contrary, they are rumored to be a nation of people with a very formal way of interacting, in private as well as in business. At least this was my perception prior to my short assignment in Munich. To a large degree, this time perception and reality matched. An example; a female executive in the hotel was married to another senior department head, and whenever they communicated with each other, in front of other employees, they addressed each other with "Herr" and "Frau"; "Good Afternoon Herr X, how are you doing? said Frau X, I am fine Frau X, said Herr X". Must be the definition of being ultra-formal.

Most often the perception of an unknown destination and culture is correct, at least parts of it. However, it does not matter how much homework you have done, you will be hit by surprises. Make sure to be humble and open to whatever is coming your way and embrace the culture as being yours.

Think Global, Act Local

To me, this expression is far more than a cliché. Bring along, and draw on your experiences, whilst constantly adapting to the new environment. Have this in mind, whilst using common sense, and it will assist you in having a smooth transition to most new cultures.

Let me exemplify this with a few memories. Nothing extraordinary, just a few anecdotes experienced in not-too-familiar working environments.

The first one is from Hammamet, Tunisia. It relates to a specific dealing with the local bank office. Our relationship with the senior people of the bank was very good. Amongst others, the financing of the renovation had been arranged through the branch office in Hammamet. One Friday afternoon, never to forget, Hedi, our Director of Finance, came to my office looking very serious and concerned. Straight to the point, he told me that the paychecks that had been distributed the same day to the members of the entire staff and were due to be cashed on the Monday following the weekend, would not be honored by the bank. Our credit facility was simply too much overdrawn. I was surprisingly calm and collected and asked Hedi to call the bank manager and invite him and his closest colleagues for a few beers. I was hopeful that this, more than awkward, situation could be solved face-to-face. If not, we were looking at a true disaster.

Friday afternoon and you ask the bank manager to pass by for a few beers. This can work in Hammamet, but most probably not in the European business world. When I say, "This can work," I mean that the bank manager and his colleagues happily leave their office early, and an hour after the phone call enjoy the first beer. We convinced the bankers that our backlog of business was very healthy, and that our cash flow in a not too distant future would resolve this unfortunate financial situation. The salary checks were all cashed on the Monday and luckily our prediction for the future was correct.

I would never have acted the way I did, had the same situation occurred shortly after my arrival to Tunisia, though I do not know what I would have done. After three years, I had grown accustomed to my new business environment and acted accordingly.

In Soma Bay, Egypt, the closest airport is the one in Hurghada, an hour away. This is where I experienced an interesting "power exhibition" of the sort that you would hardly encounter at Heathrow Airport, or in any major airport in the world. Once, before leaving for the airport, our Security Manager asked if I had time to meet up with the airport's Security Manager before boarding the flight to Cairo. This is a man who had helped us in the past, especially with VIP arrivals, though I had never met him in person, and the tighter band we can establish, the better. You never know when this friendship can come in handy. Unfortunately, I arrived a bit late to the airport, however I was expected and escorted to some kind of VIP room for the meeting with the man in question. After a ten-minute wait, I became conscious of the risk of missing the flight. In he came, impeccably dressed in his newly pressed uniform. His entourage left, only the tea boy stayed on. There we were, looking at each other, he, not speaking a word of English, I, not speaking a word of Arabic. Smiling, smiling, smiling, and drinking sweet, very sweet tea. I tried to explain, by pointing to my watch, that I was running late. Smile. As per the timetable, the plane had now taken off. Another tea, and my friend escorted me to a car, both of us in the back seat, for transport over the tarmac to the awaiting plane, and awaiting crew and impatient passengers in a full cabin. He escorted me onto the plane, and we hugged each other as close friends do.

Why this theatre? He exhibited his power by instructing the plane to wait until he gave clearance. He was the King of the airport and for him, I was, if not the King, the Prince of a nice resort. We could surely, if needed, take advantage of one another's services. Fine with me!

Sometimes, the best is to do nothing, not to destabilize the existing equilibrium. Outside the main gate of the Sheraton Grande Laguna Phuket, over the years, a taxi stand had been established. Not a regular taxi stand, but private cars, not always very nice, with, not always very nice drivers. It was a bad first impression to our guests, and I was, shortly after my arrival, determined to "beautify" the welcome experience. As a master of delegation, I asked our Security Manager to nicely explain to the drivers that there were new instructions from the new management, and basically, they could pack and leave for good. How naïve can you be? A few days later, in front of the hotel entrance, I was confronted by a 2-meter, 110 kg person. Not many of those in Thailand. He looked down at me and, in good English, he explained that he was the "the boss of the taxis." Then he asked about my wife and two kids. That was enough for me to leave the taxi friends alone for quite some time. I also stayed away from another eyesore, all the local vendors on the beach. It should be stressed that it doesn't work to contact the authorities as they are fully aware of the situation.

Acting locally sometimes means to stay away and not act at all.

The Sheraton Istanbul was located by Taksim Park, and the entrance of the hotel faced a very busy street where the traffic was controlled by the police. Usually the same, very polite, gentleman made sure that the flow of cars was as smooth as ever possible. However, when it was time for my wife Helle, with Victor in the pram, to cross the street he didn't care about the flow of the traffic. He made sure to immediately stop all traffic and give time and space for my two family members to safely cross over. In the beginning, Helle felt embarrassed, but quite fast grew accustomed to this extraordinary service. With 30-40 policemen daily having free lunch in our staff canteen, this was a nice courtesy from the police force.

The Menu

The heart of any culture is food. The good thing

is that wherever you end up, there will always be some dishes to your liking. In chronological order, let me list what has made a lasting culinary impression.

Over the last two decades, Sweden has become internationally known for its vast number of outstanding restaurants, however in the context of my journey, I must mention a traditional Swedish dish, meatballs (köttbullar). To be served with mashed potatoes (potatismos), cream sauce, and lingonberries.

As a Swede, being used to daily hot food for lunch, I could never grow accustomed to the Norwegian cold sandwiches as the mid-day meal. Overall, I am sorry to say that the Norwegian food culture did not leave a big impression on me. However, the Norwegian salmon is world class.

Already during my time in Cyprus (1988 -1990), I was introduced to the Middle Eastern kitchen. The Sheraton Limassol was owned by a Lebanese family, and the "fine dining" of the hotel was a Lebanese restaurant. I fell in love with the food. Meze with hummus, tabbouleh, falafel... You name it, I'll eat it!

Portugal might not be famous for its food, but I could easily have my favorite Portuguese dish 2-3 times a week; Chicken Piri Piri. Not in any random restaurant, you must find the right place, like "Rei do Frango" in Guia, Algarve. You round off the meal with a Bica (the Portuguese equivalent to espresso) and a Macieria or two. Macieira is a Portuguese brandy, not the smoothest, but perfect after the spicy marinated chicken. Let me quote my Norwegian friend Morten, who fully appreciated a Macieira now and then; "A *Bica Brutal* is a Bica without Macieira, a *Bica Normal* is a Bica with Macieira, a *Bica Optimal* is a Macieira without Bica!" (This should be said in a Norwegian / Portuguese accent).

To Turkey and kebab and fantastic meze again.

The couscous in Tunisia is outstanding, and not to forget the Tunisian brik, which is a whole egg in a triangular filo pastry pocket with chopped onion, tuna, harissa (chili paste) and parsley.

Om Ali, a bread pudding, and a national dessert of Egypt was the kids' favorite.

Jordan and more meze and Mansaf, the traditional dish of Jordan. It's made of lamb in a sauce of fermented dried yogurt. It's served in a casserole with layers of rice, vegetables, and lamb meat.

It's hard to describe the food of Thailand, from

street food to Michelin star restaurants, you have it all. I cannot imagine a cuisine with more and better variation, and for me, a fan of spicy food, it is just unbeatable. Watch out so you don't lose your taste buds for eternity; spicy is a relative term, and spicy for a Thai is far different from spicy for a Westerner. "Farang spicy," i.e., spicy for a foreigner, is good enough if you like hot food. Pad Thai (Stir Fried Noodles), Kaeng Lueang (Yellow Curry), Khao Soi (Coconut Curry Noodle Soup), Tom Yum Goong (Hot & Sour Shrimp Soup), just a few favorites.

I think that, amongst most Westerners, there is a big misperception of what Chinese food is all about. I had a wake-up call in Hong Kong, where I was introduced to the authentic Chinese kitchen. Arriving in Hong Kong in 2011, I was a big fan of Chinese food, i.e., what I considered to be the Chinese kitchen. Years back, during my two years in Gothenburg, the favorite Sunday dinner took place at Lai Wa, the best Chinese Restaurant in town. I knew my dinner numbers on the menu by heart: 16, 28, 29, 47 plus rice and a Coke. These are great dishes, but I dare say that most coming out of the kitchen is not authentic Chinese food. It's "Europeanized" to please the palate of a laowai (foreigner). This is most probably the case in most Chinese restaurants outside Asia. At the Regal

Airport Hotel in Hong Kong, we had seven restaurants, of which two were Chinese, one Cantonese and one Shanghainese. I was not adventurous enough to fully dig into the variety of Chinese food, which I regret. I usually stuck to my non-adventurous favorites, e.g., spring rolls, dim sum, roast duck, steamed oysters in ginger and garlic. What often discouraged me was the texture of many dishes, much like jellyfish.

Despite my earlier comments about the Norwegian lunch sandwiches, I must highlight the Danish open-faced sandwiches, smørrebrød, which has become a national dish. For eight months in 2012/2013, I worked in southern Sweden, whilst living with the family in Copenhagen. Minimum once a week I enjoyed smørrebrød, every time with different toppings. The sandwich is built on a thin layer of dense sourdough rye bread with a vast variety of toppings. Smørrebrød is eaten in only one order: herring first, followed by other fish, then meat, then cheese. Whenever in Denmark, smørrebrød is a must.

Wining and dining is an important part of being a hotelier. Enjoy it to the fullest!

Service delivery

The biggest difference in getting used to working in the Middle East and Asia, compared to Europe, is not that the weekend starts on a Friday in the Middle East or that you often have an official six-day working week in Asia. You will also soon grow accustomed to the various holidays and traditions. This is one of the beauties of being an "expatriate nomad." As a hotelier, by far the most enjoyable difference is that you are in the position to deliver first-class service, thanks to lower labor costs. After ten years in the Middle East and Asia, I had an eight-month stint back in my home country, Sweden. From Asia with low cost of labor, to streamlined staffing in Sweden. I am still proud of changing the garbage handler and saving some dollars for the hotel in Helsingborg. Hardly the working task of a GM in Hong Kong, Thailand, or Jordan. Back to reality and a good wake-up call! The influence and power of the union was another strong wake-up call.

I sometimes use the following comparison: if you want to give the guests in Sweden the opportunity to have an orange juice in the lobby at check-in, just place a vending machine close to the reception desk. In Thailand, you have two nicely dressed ladies serving complimentary freshly squeezed orange juice to all arriving guests. As a first impression, that's a bit of a difference.

The conclusion is simple: if you want to provide luxury service, with a healthy bottom line, it's far more demanding to operate a hotel in Europe than in Asia, or in the Middle East.

What I have learned

Preparation for an unknown culture. Take your time and study your upcoming destination as thoroughly as possible. The more you know, the faster and easier you will settle in, and the more appreciated you will be. A lack of knowledge about non-familiar culture might "backfire." To adapt smoothly, be as open-minded as possible.

Perception is reality until proven wrong. Watch out, be aware that you initially might have an incorrect perception of a new culture.

There are "no-nos" in all cultures. Make sure not to learn them the hard way.

You are the Guest. Your co-workers will act, and react, differently from what you are used to. Even though you want to implement your way of running the hotel, make sure to first familiarize yourself firmly with the new business environment and culture. You are the guest, act accordingly, be humble and be respectful.

Think global but act local should be the "base philosophy" even if it means that you at occasions have to adopt "think local and act local".

You are the Role Model. More so in the Middle East and Asia, than in Europe. As GM, your behavior is being scrutinized 24/7 by all associates. Nothing more needs to be said.

Language. Make a strong effort to pick up the new language. A few pre-arrival sentences will also work wonders.

Corruption and Bribes. Play safe, don't do anything stupid, not even marginally stupid.

Feelings. "People will forget what you said, people will forget what you did, but people will never forget how you made them feel."

Take advantage of a different food culture. Be it tom yum goong or jellyfish—try it all!

Luxury service is often related to the number of associates. Especially in Asia, with low labor costs, you are spoiled as GM. It's a tougher test in Europe to provide true luxury service, with an acceptable bottom line.

DAY-TO-DAY OPERATIONS

The Employer

Your job as GM is obviously affected by the involvement of your boss and by the entity being your employer. The reporting line is straight forward when you work directly for an owner. However, when you work for a hotel operated by a management company, it's a different "ball game." In short, in good times, no worries, your salary is covered in the monthly P&L. In bad times, during the COVID-19 pandemic as an example, and your hotel is running in red figures, the owner must inject funds for the ongoing operations of the hotel.

The above highlights the relationship between the management company, represented by the GM, and the owning company, usually represented by an asset manager. A hotelier representing a management company would benefit from a thorough course in diplomacy, and maybe even in negotiations, before experiencing the first role as GM. It's often a tough balance to keep the two parties satisfied, one on your left shoulder, and the other one on the right. The GM signs a "letter of appointment" with the management company, but I can assure you that you will often be reminded of who the owner is, by the owner and by your corporate boss! The "golden rule": achieve the financial goals of the hotel, and you will be left in peace by both parties (see further, "OWNER RELATIONS"). As GM, one of the best compliments that you can receive from the corporate executives of the management company is: "That GM is very good with owners." The worst that can happen, is to have the reputation of "being in the pocket of the owner". It's often a thin line to walk, and the importance of the balancing act cannot be underestimated.

After 15 years as GM with ITT Sheraton/Starwood, I was, in 2011, for the first time working directly for an owner, as GM of the Regal Airport Hotel in Hong Kong. How nice to only have one party to satisfy, and to worry about. However, one issue is that, by default, you and the owner will disagree on certain aspects of the operation and you, as GM, have limited space to act and react. In the end, you'll make sure to keep your job, and you will adhere to the wishes of the owner. If you have the management company on one shoulder, it's easier to take a disagreement. You can, on some occasions, refer to and "hide behind" corporate standards and policies and procedures. If necessary, you will hopefully also have the support of your corporate boss.

I had a hard time adjusting to the direct line to the owner. Many times, I felt like a "puppet," only being in my position to be a nice guy and to abide by the instructions from the owner. I soon learned that this is common in Asia. It was a contributing factor in my decision to leave Hong Kong, after only 18 months.

Business Hotel vs. Resort

Nothing can be compared to a busy business hotel!

At the Regal Airport Hotel in Hong Kong and at the Anantara Riverside in Bangkok, we had a lot of business travelers, however it was mixed with a good number of leisure travelers. My only time as GM of a "pure business hotel", though with few leisure guests, was at the Sheraton Amman Al Nabil Hotel & Towers, 2002-2005. A newly built, beautiful 5-star hotel in the center of town. The great part was not only that we were daily running high occupancy, but it was also the mix of guests that you experience in such a hotel. Individual business travelers, international conference attendees, high-profile delegations, plus local patrons enjoyed the bars and restaurants. Around 5:00 pm I used to stroll around in the lobby to inhale the atmosphere. The lobby would be full of guests coming back from their daily business meetings, and the lobby bar would start filling up; it was a fantastic buzz—the hotel was pumping! On numerous occasions, I was thinking: "This is why I became a hotelier." Even as an asset manager, many years later, at the InterContinental Hotel in Hong Kong, I sometimes spent 15-20 minutes in the lobby in the late afternoon, just to feel the pulse.

"It is more demanding to be GM in a business hotel than a resort," is a common perception. On the contrary, I firmly believe that it is the other way around.

The business traveler is expecting nothing but top service and a smooth stay whilst on a business trip, otherwise the guest will stay with the competition the next time in town. Maybe they will give the hotel a second chance, but no more, assuming the guest doesn't prefer to stay with you due to the convenience of the location. Regardless of the experience, the stay will end up on an expense voucher and not on a private credit card statement. The average length of stay in a business hotel is normally around two nights. What can go wrong in this short period of time for the guest not to come back? It's not a given, but let's assume courteous, well-groomed, and serviced-minded associates. If the cleanliness is perfect, the breakfast is of top quality with a nice spread, there are some good dining options, including timely room service and a nice bar plus a well-equipped gym and a smooth check-in/out process (digital or face-to-face), a comfortable bed and reliable, fast wi-fi – the guest will come back. In the "pre-mobile phone era," we would have had to add timely message service and timely wake-up calls. There are obviously other challenges, however if these basics can be delivered, we will not lose guests and we will generate repeaters. It's not simple, but it's not rocket science, it's certain basics that must be available and well delivered.

The same applies to resorts, however, "the basics" are tougher to define. Not forgetting that the invoice will be paid by private, hard-earned, taxed money. The average length of stay will be around five nights and assuming all is in perfect order as described for a business hotel, there are so many more services and preferences that must be in line with the guests' expectations during a longer period, that's the big challenge.

Preferences and likings differ: the location of the room/suite (sea view, close to pool or beach or the restaurants), quality and quantity of sunbeds by the pools and the beach, the chlorine level of the water in the pools, the games, activities and opening hours of the kids' club, the presence of mosquitos and other insects, variety of restaurants and kids' menu, too many kids, not enough lifeguards on the beach, not the latest water sports equipment, the fragrance of the spa treatment oil, it goes on and on. I had a guest who strongly complained about the pin placement on the greens at the nearby golf course. Even better, an elderly female guest in Phuket once complained about too much sun (!).

One point is that the guest normally is more demanding in a resort, in addition the working conditions for the GM are tougher than in a business hotel. The hotel industry is far more than normal office hours, and we all need time off to charge our batteries. In a business hotel, occupancy is normally lower on weekends and public holidays and with the right set-up of a duty manager roster during these periods, the GM can have some off time for relaxation. The GM in a resort does often not have the same privilege. It's well exemplified by my time in Amman, and it is also applicable in the other resorts where I served as GM.

Drive about an hour "down the hill" from Amman and you'll arrive at the Dead Sea (the lowest point on earth) with several nice resorts. This is where my family and our friends occasionally spent long weekends and public holidays. We would always stay at the Marriott, having the same owner as the Sheraton in Amman. The Marriott was usually packed with a mix of international guests and the Amman socialites. Every single time, during four years with numerous visits, the GM, Philip Papadopoulos, was visible to the guests. Of course, a full resort with guests paying high rates, he was working and expected to be there by the guests, his staff and the owner. The GM of the business hotel relaxing by the pool, whilst the resort GM going full speed – a big, big difference. In a resort a GM is expected to be seen, and interact with the guests, far more than in a business hotel. Sometimes you feel as if the main objective of some guests is to have as much time as possible with the GM. To top it up, I do not know how many of my kids' school holidays coincided with the high season of "my resort", i.e., no way to spend the full vacation with the family.

In late 2010 I was in-between jobs, on the couch and golf courses in Phuket, awaiting my move to Hong Kong with Regal Hotels. I was then asked by Starwood, my previous employer, if I could take on a short assignment as Interim Cluster GM of the two Starwood resorts in the Maldives, W and Sheraton, awaiting the permanent GM. One month, but only one month, in the Maldives, impossible not to accept. W, where I stayed, is a stunning resort situated on a small atoll. It took exactly eight minutes to walk around the entire little island. The guests arrived by seaplane, and all were greeted on the jetty by the GM and team. This meant that every single guest knew who the GM was and, whether you liked it or not, it was constant interaction with the guests, and nowhere "to hide." After three weeks, Helle and the kids came to visit, and life became a bit more normal. The one month in the Maldives was a fantastic experience, especially the 5-star+ W, but I can honestly say that it was a very nice feeling to take off in the seaplane after the mission was completed. I have a lot of respect for GMs who stay for many years in this environment.

It sounds magical, but to me it is a real hardship assignment.

There are always exceptions, but I will again conclude that it is more demanding to be GM of a resort than a business hotel. I would also say that you will be the outright winner if you laser focus on, and consistently deliver the basics (!), being in the business hotel or in the resort.

Meetings

Let's face it, conducting a meaningful and productive meeting is a difficult task.

I have not experienced a hotel that hasn't had a "Morning Meeting." This meeting is tough to chair, as it has a tendency to become a bit boring and monotonous, however it's really "a necessary evil." Feedback from yesterday, the main issue for the day – arrivals, F&B functions, maintenance projects, site inspections and so on. We all, usually GM, Hotel Manager / Resident Manager, and department heads, need to communicate clearly in a way that all concerned know the priorities for the coming 24 hours. A not uncommon "disease" is that some individuals around the table hear, but they do not listen (!), instead they are simply waiting for their turn to say something (not always of importance). The reality is that, at this time of the working day, all participants are not always 100% in top shape and up to speed. For many years as GM, I was chairing the morning meeting, however I later found it beneficial to rotate the chairmanship amongst all participants on a weekly basis. The experience of sitting in *the Chair* for a week and supervising the meeting also meant a more focused participant going forward. My aim was always to keep the morning meeting short and sharp, i.e., ideally 30 minutes, max 45 minutes. I used to know hotels with morning meetings daily lasting up to two hours. To me, this is nothing but mismanagement. I once had a tour of the Venetian Macau (3,000 suites, gaming, mega food and beverage operation, huge function space and vast retail) by the Front Office Manager. I was curious and asked about their morning meeting: 40 people in a one-hour meeting. "How is this managed?" I asked. "If you have nothing important to say, you say nothing." I couldn't agree more.

When I joined the Anantara Riverside in Bangkok, the morning meeting took place when the breakfast service was at its busiest. The meeting started at 09.00 hrs. and was soon changed to 08.00 hrs. Not a popular decision, but it didn't make sense to be stuck in a meeting room when the hotel operation was in full swing. Often this is the best time for GM and management to walk around and meet the guests before they go off to work or on outings for the day. It's also good for staff to see the management present at a very busy time of the day, when they can offer support where needed. In Langkawi, there was also a short "3 pm meeting" due to flight schedules to the island, with a lot of changes and late arrivals. In both cases it was a question of adapting the timing of the meeting to the operations.

There are daily, weekly and monthly departmental meetings, some more important than others. For the GM to constantly be up to date with the activities of the sales department and the revenue management process is of utmost importance, and I will tackle this separately. It is vital for department heads to be able to analyze the financial performance of their own department, and to be able to communicate this to their colleagues in a clear and understandable way. For the key people to be aware of the overall financial status of the hotel is a top priority. Therefore, to me, the gathering of the highest priority is a monthly P&L meeting. This meeting can be conducted in many ways, however most important is the involvement of the department heads and the meeting not to become a one-way communication by the GM and/or the Director of Finance. I found it most productive when the departmental figures were distributed as soon as they were finalized, and then the respective department head had 4-5 working days to review and analyze the figures, as well as to check with the finance department if something was not clear. This also gave everyone time, prior to the actual P&L meeting, not only to analyze the past month and year-to-date figures, but as important, to establish an action plan going forward. This way, a good understanding amongst department heads is created and the importance and contribution from all concerned becomes vital. The GM's role is to summarize and give a very clear picture of the overall "state of affairs" and to highlight the actions and priorities for each department, and for the hotel as a combined business unit. Figures, figures, figures! One of the important roles of a GM is to chair the meeting in such a way that the figures make sense to all participants and to make sure that this important meeting doesn't become too "dry." A bit of humor has never hurt.

Another meeting of importance is an external one, though prepared internally, the yearly budget presentation. During two years as Area GM with

Minor Hotels, 2013-215, I also got accustomed to the "warm-up meetings," i.e., the quarterly reviews. These meetings were as important as the budget presentation. The "beauty" of these meetings was that all your peers, together with everyone from the corporate office with a respectable title, were attending the individual presentations, i.e., always a three-digit number of participants. The most comprehensive template that I have ever experienced had been worked on and prepared for weeks. This was the time to exhibit your detailed knowledge of your hotel's figures and the status versus the competition.

In some strange way, I personally thrived on these meetings, I enjoyed it. I was fortunate to have smart and reliable GMs under my "area umbrella," and I could well "defend" the figures of my own hotel. It was a bit of: "Hit me if you can, I know my shit!" One thing is for sure, it's based on these kinds of meetings that the corporate executives form their opinion about you as a hotelier. The Minor quarterly – and budget reviews are famous for being tough. If the Chairman, Bill Heinecke, got his teeth into one hotel, he wouldn't let go and it was like a "cart blanche" for the other executives at the head table to put the GM in question on the BBQ. Tough questions, sometimes in combination with not enough homework, resulted in some GMs sweating in the heat whilst being grilled until they were more than well-done. However, no doubt that the way these reviews are conducted, the way participants are pushed outside their comfort zone, help all to grow as hoteliers. Not surprisingly, Minor GMs are after sought and considered to be a great catch for any hotel company of high standards.

What I appreciate about budget presentations is the preparation. It forces you to review and analyze the business in every detail and set a refined strategy for the future. The monthly P&L meetings are a good basis for all concerned to actively contribute to the budget preparation.

At the actual budget review, before getting into the analysis of figures, make sure to present your strategy for the coming year. Ideally, calm and collected, you should display a thorough knowledge of the marketplace, i.e., the different feeder markets, existing and upcoming competition, macroeconomics that will influence your figures, positive and negative. Be in control of the presentation—"offence is the best defense." Be stubborn, show that you believe in your figures, supported by a well-thought-out strategy!

I learned the hard way how NOT to present a

budget. During my Sheraton days, the budget template was 8/4, i.e., 8 months of actual figures for the current year plus 4 months forecast. The budget for the coming year was based on, and compared with, the current year and a "classic" was to "sandbag" the last quarter of the current year. In Marrakesh, at my second budget review as GM of Sheraton Hammamet, I made such a strong case of a disastrous last quarter of the year that my boss, Sami Zoghbi, then President for Sheraton Africa & Middle East, simply said: "If this is correct, then your budgeted figures for next year are too strong. Make sure to redo your budget!" That was it, the end of the meeting. One shouldn't forget that the individuals reviewing your figures, at least in some cases, are as smart as you are, and occasionally even smarter.

My biggest contribution to a budget presentation was in 2013 whilst working for Minor Hotels. At the Anantara Riverside we had an F&B promotion at the time of the budget reviews, "Octoberfest." To create a genuine atmosphere, the sausages and beer were accompanied by a German brass band. You can imagine the faces of all attendees of the budget reviews, which took place at the corporate head office, when in the middle of a presentation, the doors of the big conference room open and a 4-piece brass band enters, playing in full blast with service staff of the hotel handing out promotional flyers. A bit of a risk, but it was well received.

Cleanliness

During my time with Starwood in the Asia / Pacific region, there was a policy to once a year engage an Australian company called The Environmental Health Consultancy (EHC), which specialized in food safety inspections and advising the hotels on how to improve on this important aspect of the operations. The results of the inspections were copied to the corporate office and not scoring high would be a big embarrassment and obviously reflected negatively on your professionalism as a hotelier. The MD of the referred company, Kirwin Hamman, is a very nice person with whom I had a good personal relation, however he would never "put a blind eye" to anything not to his liking that should be included in his report and rating of the hotel. In 2007, such a food safety inspection took place at the Sheraton Grande Laguna Phuket and was conducted by Kirwin. Due to my curiosity, and thanks to our "sophisticated intelligence service" (also used towards visiting VIPs and bosses) I, at any given moment, knew the whereabouts of Kirwin and at least I got a feeling for the progress of the inspection.

What seems to be totally unrelated to a food safety inspection, is that we had two “house elephants”, Yum Yum and Ning Nong. They lived in the “Elephant Park” close to the Sheraton and daily, together with their “mahoot” (wrangler), they walked through the gardens of the resort to the beach where they had “cool off sessions” in the Andaman Sea. It was a fantastic, and unique, experience to the amusement of our guests, especially the children. Also daily, Yum Yum and Ning Nong came to the receiving bay of the hotel to have a nice meal, usually old fruit, and other leftover food. The dots were coming together... I received a call that Kirwin was checking an area back of the house and I thought it was time to pass by for a friendly chat. Whilst talking to Kirwin, I spotted over his shoulders Yum Yum and Ning Nong having their daily gourmet meal on the receiving bay! How to rescue the situation? Impossible, I burst out in laughter and asked Kirwin to turn around to the most unique view he had ever experienced whilst making a hotel food safety inspection. I promised him that this would be the last supper on the receiving bay for our "house elephants." One thing is for sure, it was an unforgettable moment for both Kirwin and me.

In the January of 2011 I joined Regal Hotels in Hong Kong as GM of the Regal Airport Hotel, a 1,100-room "monster" directly connected to terminal 1 of the airport. Prior to my arrival I had proudly stolen a piece of business from Marriott, our main competitor close to the airport. Nigel Peters, a close friend from Phuket, and part-owner of the event company Midas Promotions, staged Justin Bieber in May 2011 at the AsiaWorld–Arena, very close to the airport. Bieber himself stayed downtown, but his crew, musicians, and technicians stayed with us at the Regal Hotel. Upon arrival, the crew members left all their private luggage in a conference room close to the lobby and rushed straight away to set up for the concert. So far so good. I really enjoyed watching the performance with Nigel, standing 10 meters from the stage - a great experience for a "tone-deaf" old man. At around 23.00 hrs. I got a phone call to my apartment in the hotel. It was the always calm and humble Nigel, who explained that there was a problem. The luggage of the crew was nowhere to be found and the atmosphere in the lobby was "a bit tense". I, maybe not as calm and humble as Nigel, was greeted in the lobby by Bieber's manager who, in very colorful words, explained how utterly useless our staff was, and he also explicitly expressed my value (zero minus). Luckily, shortly thereafter the luggage was found, and I could sleep without nightmares, they materialized the following morning....

Saturdays were usually days of relaxation plus some time in the office to clean up the inbox. I found one urgent message with the famous red exclamation mark. Correct, from "my friend" of the previous evening. If the experience of Friday night was unpleasant, it was a beautiful dream compared to the reading of this email. It was a very well-worded message that first described the mess that we had created the day of arrival, and then came the crescendo. With the support of photos that were attached, he pointed out that we had bed bugs in the guest rooms and two of his staff members had suffered from bites, illustrated by his photos. He went on to say that this information would soonest be communicated to local media, Hong Kong Tourist Board and the owners of the hotel. I immediately answered his email and politely asked for time to investigate the matter and promised to revert within 48 hours – he accepted. I was fortunate to have our Executive Housekeeper living in the hotel and during a brief meeting, I explained the situation and the urgency at hand. I insisted on having written confirmation from two independent pest control companies within 36 hours stating that there were no bed bugs in the guest rooms that the manager referred to.

As it transpired, we did not have any bed bugs, but some other small creatures in the wall-to-wall carpets. I got my requested letters on time and composed the best well-crafted email in my life, which generated a quick response of acceptance from, at this stage, my dear friend. How to deal with complaints is a separate issue, how to deal with not properly cleaned guest rooms is even more important. With the short length of stay in an airport hotel, we could fast empty, and seal off, the entire floor for smoke treatment and deep cleaning. We went floor by floor and we could go back to normal operation quite fast. The described experience highlights the utmost importance of detailed cleaning procedures and checks. I would also say that if you can ever influence the interior design of a guest room, avoid wall-to-wall carpets.

In the past, cleanliness might not have been on the absolute top of the agenda for some hoteliers. However, the COVID-19 pandemic put the importance of cleanliness and hygiene in the focus of all hoteliers and more importantly, in the focus of all guests.

Guest Interaction/Recognition

A natural part of being a hotelier is to interact with your guests, this is the evident way of obtaining feedback. If you are not "around and about," you will lose touch, not only with your associates, but also with the service and facilities that you provide for the guests. To be a bit of an exhibitionist helps.

One should never underestimate the importance of the first – and last impression. If you do not feel welcome at check-in, or at the first point of contact, it can take quite some time for the hotel to "recover" this first experience. It is even worse if the guest leaves with a "bad taste" due to a negative last encounter. In Langkawi, most of our guests left for the airport with transport arranged by the resort, hence we knew when to expect the guests at the airport. Even if the farewell at the resort had been nice and the guests left happy, we made sure to surprise them with a final positive touch. We had the airport manned, not only to welcome guests, but also to assist in making sure that the airport check-in was hassle-free. After the check-in, wishes for a pleasant flight, and a nice give-away from the resort were handed to the guests by a member of our airport guest service staff. Last impression – guest recognition!

At the Sheraton Amman, we went all out to make sure to have as much guest contact as possible. We had very nice sit-down check-in counters in the lobby, and next to them, we put an extra desk for the management. I, as GM, and Francois Waller, Resident Manager, took turns to "beautify" this desk in the mornings and late afternoons. Now and then we missed out on our "lobby desk duty", but overall, it was an initiative much appreciated by our guests, as well as by the associates of the hotel. The obvious advantage was that we picked up a lot of feedback. Most importantly, to be able to deal with, and act upon, occasional negative comments. An important fact is that not only most hotel guests, but people in general, are a bit vain, i.e., they enjoy being recognized in a hotel, ideally recognized by the GM.

When hosting meetings and conferences in the hotel, not only should the participants be well looked after, but also the people in charge of the event. I always carried the daily function sheet in my jacket, so I knew when and where coffee breaks and meals took place. Like this, I made sure to pass by, not only to check that all was in good order, but it gave me the opportunity to meet up with the organizer and key people of the conference. Often you would then be introduced to the most senior person, the MD, or the CEO of the company in question. I can assure you that all concerned much appreciate the fact that the GM of the hotel shows interest in the meeting. This "indirect sales" works wonders. It's also important for the GM to participate in the feedback/evaluation meeting following a conference. The GM's involvement will generate a lot of repeat business, it is as simple as that. (See further, "SALES and MARKETING") It's a question of guest recognition.

The GM can do a part, but the big impression comes from the guest contact staff. The department heads can, for example, drill the fact that guest names should be used, which is often the best and most efficient guest recognition, but ultimately it comes from the attitude of the individual staff member. It starts with the recruiting process.

There is also something that could be referred to as "negative guest interaction" that most of us have experienced. These are situations where you feel mistreated as a guest, often not because of non-friendly service, but due to technology.

I was once doing a bit of research on hotels in Singapore and, at one hotel, I asked about the room rate at the reception desk. I felt that the rate was very high, which I told the lady behind the desk, who answered: "If you log in on the PC across the lobby, you can find cheaper rates online." How can you allow technology to override your rate strategy (if there was any)?

In a restaurant in Amsterdam, I asked them to make a reservation for the following week. "Have you checked online?" What a nice greeting! I could not make the table reservation at the restaurant because they insisted on a deposit as a guarantee, and this could only be done online. How can you allow technology to contribute to potentially losing business?

SOPs and Regulations

SOPs – Standard Operating Procedures. It's so boring that I should leave this subject blank! Are SOPs needed or are they restricting the way we do business? The answer is that we do need them, especially in areas where we handle money and areas of safety and security concerns. With the risk of being misunderstood, I used to say, sometimes maybe too loud, that SOPs are there to be disobeyed. What I was trying to convey was that there should be room for flexibility, that associates should be allowed to "think outside the box", i.e., you can deviate from an SOP if it makes common sense. It is important that the associates have been empowered in a way that they feel comfortable and secure to take advantage of common sense instead of a rigid SOP.

A perfect example of how to be rigid and unnecessarily adhere to an SOP: together with friends, I occasionally visited one of the best restaurants by the Chao Phraya River in Bangkok. Good food and drinks and total relaxation. Even in busy Bangkok you can truly wind down. One Saturday, at 5.00 pm sharp, a waiter informs us that we must leave, as this was now the deadline for wearing shorts on the terrace. Two hours of wining and dining, and we are asked to leave. Common sense was most probably flushed down in the dirty river and the SOP prevailed. I haven't been back since.

The most important SOPs are not the ones relating to the set-up of a room service trolley or how to greet a guest, but the ones relating to avoiding tragic incidents or actions to be taken in case of such an incident.

In a resort, important SOPs mean adhering to rules and regulations related to safety by the pools and the beach. Surprisingly, this is sometimes a weak point. If the resort is part of a chain, always check that you are in line with corporate guidelines, then double-check with your insurance company. This also applies to all recreational areas, be it the health club, spa or the kids' playground. If not a chain hotel, make sure to have the insurance company advise and sign off on your signage, rules and regulations, as well as the number, locations, and timing of staffing.

A special aspect of the morning meetings that we implemented at the Sheraton Amman was to regularly review and update our procedures in case of a crisis, e.g., a bomb threat or natural disaster. Amongst others, this included who and when to print the in-house guest list. This was done three times a day and stored, together with walkie-talkies and a video recorder, in a dedicated place outside the hotel. We also confirmed meeting points for key members of staff, who would be the liaison person with the authorities, contact person for the media, where to set up press conferences, who to contact at the corporate office and much more to act on, in case of a crisis. It was a detailed procedure that we also tested with "dry runs."

A tragedy took place in Amman in the evening of November 9, 2005. Three hotels were hit by suicide bombers, causing the death of 60 people and 115 injured. It doesn't matter which SOPs you have in place, it's impossible to safeguard a hotel from acts of terrorism. Al-Qaeda in Iraq immediately claimed the attack on a website, saying they were trying to hit "American and Israeli intelligence and other Western European governments." (BBC 2005)

The three hotels, Grand Hyatt, Radisson SAS and Days Inn, were immediately evacuated. We had some of the Hyatt guests check in at the Sheraton and we supported blankets, food and water for guests waiting outdoors for clearance to return to their hotel rooms. With our close ties to the Grand Hyatt, we had the opportunity to make a visit to the hotel shortly after they re-opened on November 19. We had a run-down of the tragedy and the actions taken by the hotel. They were all heroes and did a fantastic job under these dreadful circumstances. We learned that there was one issue that had not been anticipated. When it was time for all evacuated guests to return to their rooms a bottleneck occurred. A large number of the guests had left the hotel without a key card and/or ID. When cleared to return, Hyatt associates had the obligation to ask for ID. Key cards had to be punched and a lot of guests had to be escorted to their room to produce identification. This was all necessary but was time-consuming and despite the tragic circumstances, some guests voiced their discontent. In those days facial recognition did not exist and to use your Apple wallet as a key card holder was unheard of.

My favorite story relating to SOPs and lack of flexibility derives from the airport in Phuket. When I was based in Bangkok, I spent the weekends in Phuket, as Helle lived and worked there. I travelled around a lot during the week, but if the Monday destination was Bangkok, I could opt either for the last TG flight on a Sunday or the Air Asia "early bird" on a Monday morning. Normally, I only had a carry-on, but this time I had my golf clubs to check in, which I had paid for online. At the Air Asia counter, I was informed that I had not paid for sports equipment, but for a suitcase. As the price for a suitcase and a golf bag was the same (!), all was OK, I thought. No, I had paid for the wrong item online, and I was therefore asked to step aside from the queue and go to a separate counter to pay for my golf bag. I refused to move and asked to see the supervisor. I was so upset that I was not even bothered about the long line with annoyed passengers behind me. After around a 10-minute wait (imagine the mode of the fellow passengers behind me) the supervisor arrived. Before I could even react, loud and clear he said: "I'm only here to say that you have to pay"! Till now I had kept myself relatively calm. Enough was enough! In quite colourful words, elaborately, and loudly, I expressed my feelings about his behavior as a "front man" representing the airline. I also had time to make a firm statement that this was the last time in my life I would fly with Air Asia. The SOP beat me! I not only paid, but I was also on the same flight again, the following Monday morning. When choosing a hotel, often the location decides, with airlines it's often the time schedule, unfortunately.

Most, if not all, hotel chains engage an independent company to conduct secret audits of the hotels. The "mystery shopper" usually stays one night and makes sure to use as many of the facilities as possible, including having two or three meals. The person will identify her- / himself at check out and will then review the findings with the GM, before the report is sent to the corporate office.

This is the ultimate test relating to the proper

implementation of SOPs, however to a certain degree it represents a paradox when hotels engage companies to conduct this kind of audits. Associates are encouraged to give personalized "genuine" service and then mystery audits are imposed on them, which mostly require scripted points to be covered on every interaction. Yes, junior associates require some kind of structure as a training ground, however once the skillset is learned there must be a transition to a more informal, however still professional way of connecting with the guests. Maybe a better way is the "No-No List" that Six Senses used to have. Instead of instructing associates what to do and what to say, this is a list informing the associates what not to do and what not to say, giving the individual associate more flexibility in how to interact with guests.

On occasions, the identity of the "inspector" will be revealed beforehand, simply by friendly colleagues emailing about the name and sometimes even a photo. A 24-hour notice can help a lot to improve on certain shortcomings and improve the rating.

Complaints

Smiling, well-groomed and service-minded associates, the department heads are all well-organized, the executive chef has received yet another accolade for outstanding food. The day-to-day operation is running smoother than ever. However, you are still hit with complaints. Very few, but still, it annoys you. Let's agree, "the non-complaint scenario" does not exist, it would be strange if it did.

If I did not receive a complaint of any sort, or no guest dissatisfaction was reported to me, in a long period of time, I would get concerned, even suspicious. My concern was that maybe the "chain of command" did not work, i.e., an associate with direct guest contact did not communicate the complaint to the supervisor or department head. Suspicious, when you know that something has not worked out as per plan, e.g., the breakfast service was not up to standard due to staff shortage. You want the associates with direct guest contact to deal with any eventual complaint, however, as GM, it is of great importance that you are informed. All department heads and supervisors being involved in the daily operation, should keep some kind of log. The sooner you know about a guest who is not satisfied, the better. Ideally you should get hold of the guest prior to check-out. This makes the whole process so much simpler. Even when the problem has been resolved, a contact by the GM is worth a lot, and should take place as often as feasible. Frankly, the best person to deal with a complaint is the GM. Towards the guest, and your associates, this indicates a true concern from the management and could well be the act that saves a repeat guest or generates a new one. The business card presented by the GM and "Please contact me directly when you plan your next trip" can do wonders. Again, it is a matter of guest recognition.

"My steak is not medium rare," "Not enough meatballs for my son." Complaints relating to food can usually be dealt with fast and efficiently in a polite way. The aim should always be to turn the complainer into your best friend. Without hesitation, serve the kid another five meatballs and top it up with a complimentary ice cream and the whole family will leave the restaurant with a big smile. However, it's often demanding for a waiter to handle a complaint relating to food quality as the waiter must deal with the chef in the kitchen. In the worst case, argue with the chef in the kitchen, just don't argue with the guest in the restaurant.

Wine! There are very few people that are truly knowledgeable about wine, and if they are your guests you can just hope that your wine list has the variety and quality that they deserve. However, there is an overload of guests who *think they are knowledgeable* about wine and can therefore occasionally be a bit demanding to deal with. My favorite, "the Quasi Connoisseurs", i.e., the guests *pretending to know* wine. They quickly get going at swirling the glass, raising the glass towards the light, sniffing, sniffing, sniffing, tasting, gurgling, swallowing, aaaaah! At this point they have forgotten what they have ordered and what they are tasting, which sometimes doesn't matter as they wouldn't know the difference between a light Pinot Noir and a heavy Rioja anyway. Most often you will get a nod of acceptance. If not, taste the wine in front of the guest, and if not too expensive, give the guest a compliment for having sensitive taste buds and bring another bottle. I am not questioning that wine should be tasted by the guest before being served. The guest should obviously be given the opportunity to taste what's in the bottle ordered. In addition, around 5% of all wine bottles are suffering from cork as per a true wine-loving connoisseur. If the guest, knowing wine or not, orders a bottle of Chateau Petrus for $7,000, it's a question of being proactive to avoid a potential complaint. The bottle will be opened at the guest's own risk and acceptance. Personally, I do not care what the wine label says. I am not a connoisseur or quasi-connoisseur; I just enjoy, for me, good-tasting wines.

It's a bit trickier to handle a complaint when the guest has checked out, which often is the case unfortunately. A complaint can come via many channels: reviews on reservation platforms, social media, via the corporate office, through the reservation office or even straight to your inbox. I think that complaints to be answered on any online platform should have the GM as a sign-off. There are many thoughts and studies around this subject: answer or not, who, when and how to answer. The GM might not always have time to review it all, however I firmly believe that comments from the hotel should be in the name of the GM. It shows concern, and it's also a matter of courtesy. It's a question of establishing an internal procedure for how to set it up, though a must that there is a very professional "ghost writer" for the GM. Or as some GMs do, use AI. A friend, and successful GM, said the following about AI: "I love it and I use it all the time, especially to respond to guest reviews and comments".

We often forget a fantastic way to communicate: The telephone. Use it! The best impact is created when you call a guest who has conveyed a serious complaint after having left the hotel. At the end of any severe complaint, usually the question of compensation arises. To me, the best way to deal with it is to ask the guest what would be appropriate as compensation. You would not always get an answer, but when you do, most often, the suggested compensation will be within your own "ballpark." The advantage is that the guest concludes with a feeling of satisfaction and achievement.

"Don't take it personally"! How can you not take a complaint personally? It's extremely rare that a complaint is directly related to an act of the GM, though I have to admit that it has happened to me on a couple of occasions. It doesn't matter, someone is not satisfied with what you're providing in "your hotel". The day you do not take a complaint personally, it's time to leave. If there is a complaint about a noisy A/C, it is an easy fix and all parties involved can quickly move on. However, cleanliness, food quality, service, friendliness. When these kinds of complaints occur, then you have a problem, and you better take it personally. The other side of the "complaint coin" is the compliment side. Lovely, take them personally as well, you deserve it!

There are many ways of dealing with complaints. Admitting mistakes, being honest and being trustworthy should go a long way, or as I used to say: "I have no problem pulling my pants down to the knees, then I can at least walk, however, I refuse to pull them all the way down to the ankles, impossible to walk." As we are on the human body, I remember an Australian travel writer back in 2008/2009 who in an article predicted the future of the travel industry. One of his points was that not only would TripAdvisor stand the test of time, but there would also be a future site for hoteliers to post comments about annoying and not-too-pleasant guests, "DickAdvisor."

During my short stint with Starwood in the Maldives, December 2010, I quickly realized that wining and dining was extremely expensive. The logistics to bring goods to these remote atolls cost a lot. In addition, the hoteliers take advantage of the guests not having any alternative to the bars and restaurants, isolated as they are. At the W, we had a fine-dining seafood restaurant, top class. One evening, in this restaurant, from a table of four, a gentleman stood up and approached me. He said: "Boss, coming here, I knew you were going to screw me on your prices in the restaurants, I accept that. But I do not accept that you screw me royally!" Hat off to him, well spoken. Some vodka and caviar and all in good order.

Another complaint in the Maldives. One morning, after breakfast, I passed by the pool. Three Dutch couples are in, and around, the pool. I suddenly hear: "Boss, I can see clouds in the sky today, you should buy us a drink"! They are Dutch, I said to myself, and answered the gentleman in question: "No worries, drinks on me, as much as you want." It was a busy day in the resort, and around 5 pm, I remembered my Dutch friends by the pool, "drinks on me." I cannot quantify how much they consumed, and I can luckily not remember the amount spent. It is amazing how some clouds can generate a very hefty entertainment check and some very pleased guests. This is the way to turn a complaint into a compliment!

In late 1994, as Resident Manager of the Sheraton Istanbul Hotel & Towers, I, together with Helle and baby Victor, stayed for a full month at the Hilton Hotel in Istanbul. We had closed the Sheraton for good (after renovation, it became an InterContinental franchise) though our Director of Finance and I stayed on to "clean up" and do the final hand-over to the owners. Our little family had most meals at the Hilton, and we were very well looked after. I never checked the bill during the stay, so it became a nice surprise at check-out. In those days, the procedure was a bit noisy as the bill was produced on a printer behind the reception desk. One month's accommodation and around 75 meals, the printer never stopped, and the paper was nearly at knee level of the young man who was dealing with the process. Finally, it was my turn to (pretend to) complain! I said in quite a strong voice:" It's very noisy, can you please stop the printer!" With a serious expression, he looked at me and calmly said: "Sir, the paper is complimentary." I laughed and responded, "I hope that I one day will have the privilege of working with you." I am still curious about how his hotel career developed.

Wildlife

Working in Southeast Asia for 14 years means not only being exposed to different cultures, but also to a totally different animal life than back home in Sweden, which, even though marginally, affected my hotel life.

Apart from the beautiful beach, the Sheraton

Grande Laguna Phuket was surrounded by lagoons. The most interesting creatures enjoying these lagoons were monitor lizards. Big lizards that occasionally took a stroll in the hotel gardens by the water. Very few guests were knowledgeable about the fauna of Phuket and, now and then, staff members received strong remarks that we had crocodiles (!) in the garden. The staff knew what to answer and a couple of lizards didn't bother anyone.

A triathlon race takes place annually in Phuket, with start and finish in Laguna. The race flags off on the beach for the participants to take a swim in the Andaman Sea, back to the beach, then a short run to the lagoon and a swim to the awaiting bicycles to be followed by the final run. This is a very popular triathlon, attracting competitors from all over Southeast Asia.

Back to the monitor lizards at the Sheraton - yet another guest approached the front desk staff to inform them that he had seen a crocodile by the lagoon. He received the standard answer, but this time the guest showed a video – we had a crocodile in the lagoon, the same lagoon that more than a thousand swimmers should cross ten days later! How could this be real? The only answer we could come up with was that someone from the crocodile farm on the island had planted the crocodile in the lagoon. How the creature ended up in the lagoon was at this stage of little interest. We were, together with the Laguna team, focused on how to catch the crocodile. Amongst us we had a few "crocodile knowledgeable" Aussies, but definitely no one with experience of catching crocodiles. For every day that passed, the anxiety increased. Personally, I was in a bit of a crunch. Helle was looking forward to competing in the race. What to tell her? – "Stay home because there's a crocodile waiting for you in the lagoon, but do not tell your participating friends!" We just had to catch this visitor! I think it was one of the Sheraton engineers that after a few days came up with the idea to catch the beast by setting chickens on big hooks and placing them around the lagoon. To my surprise, it worked. A one-and-a-half-meter crocodile on a chicken hook, what a relief! As an extra bonus, I can now tell Helle. Marital advice: Stay cool and wait for the right moment to tell your partner the full story (What they don't teach you at Hotel Schools!).

Next island, Langkawi, Malaysia. Two-thirds of the island is densely populated by rainforest, mangroves and foliage that are some of the oldest on the planet, and there's always the chance of spotting wild animals, however you do not want to find them in a guest room. When we, i.e., Starwood, took over the management of the hotel, one of the most frequent guest complaints related to monkeys! Monkeys that opened non-locked balcony doors and emptied whatever eatable they could find, most often they had a feast with what was left in fruit baskets. Some of them were even smart enough to open the minibar for a nice meal of Mars bars, Bounties etc. They even knew how to open beer and soda cans properly. To my astonishment, I once, through the window in my office, could see a monkey sitting in a tree crunching on chips, calmly picking one by one from a small box of Pringle chips, obviously retrieved from a guest room – what a sight! To minimize the guest complaints, we put relatively big stickers on the balcony doors, encouraging the guests to always lock the door to avoid visitors from the Langkawi wildlife. It certainly brought down the number of complaints. Sometimes it's appropriate to put some responsibility on the guests, for them to have a fully satisfactory hotel experience. Should you ever visit Langkawi for a round of golf, watch out, the monkeys can be aggressive, and they love to snatch golf balls, as well as your wallet in the golf buggy.

One early morning in Langkawi, I had a call on my mobile phone at breakfast with the following message: "Boss, there is a python in the kids' pool"! This is when the heartbeat feels dangerously high, and I quickly answered with two questions in the same sentence: "Any kids in the pool, can you catch the snake?" No and yes, and that was basically the end of the story. When I was informed that "all in good order," still with a beating heart, I did a search on the Internet: "The Reticulated Python is the largest snake on the Island, and as well as the world's longest snake. The largest captured on Langkawi was measured at 8.40m!" (Datai, n.d.)

There is a first for everything. Certain situations you have never been confronted with before and have no idea how to handle. Let more qualified people take care of the task at hand (and sincerely hope that they can catch a python!).

VIPs and VVIPs

All guests are VIPs. Even though it might be a cliché, it should be the reality. Anyway, for various reasons, some guests are treated as being more important than others. I do not think there is any other industry being so used to the "VIP concept" as the hotel industry. The VIP can be a business connection to the owner, a film – or a sports star, a travel trade executive, an important repeat guest, a journalist, the list is long. Most VIPs expect to be treated as such, i.e., greeted upon arrival by the GM, nice amenities in the room/suite, be contacted during their stay, maybe a drink. One can also make this list long, the point is that the person/s in question is on the "VIP list" for a reason and should be given extra attention. At the risk of using the term wrongly, VIPs are usually "influencers" and will often quickly spread the word about your hotel. A word of caution, some want to take advantage of their "hotel status" and ask for a bit too much. In conclusion, be nice, but not too nice. An example of being too nice, as per my wife, is to invite one or more VIPs home for dinner, which has happened on a few occasions. Helle is a teacher librarian at an international school and had the following comparison: "It would be like I invited pupils with their parents at home, and you should have the dinner prepared on time." I see her point.

There are VIPs and VVIPs. The difference is that the VVIP is of such a status that the person does not wish for attention from the management. With a few exceptions, they want to be left alone. A greeting upon arrival is expected, but that's enough. I am referring to heads of state, high diplomats, top-level musicians and actors. They always have someone in their entourage to liaise with the hotel. A polite distance, though always contactable, if needed, should be the approach towards these guests.

Over the years, I have met my fair share of VVIPs, and this will be the only section to name-drop a few. Royalties – King Abdullah and Queen Rania of Jordan, Politician – US Foreign Secretary Hillary Clinton, Diplomat – Secretary General of the UN Kofi Annan, Sports – "The Big Easy", my favorite golfer Ernie Els, Musicians – Eric Clapton, Phil Collins and Mark Knopfler together, Hollywood – Film Director and Producer Francis S Coppola.

In March 2002, US Vice President Dick Cheney visited Jordan, on his 11-nation tour in the Middle East, for talks with King Abdullah, to drum up support for the invasion of Iraq. Unprecedented security in and around the hotel. Ever since the attempted assassination of President Ronald Reagan, outside the Hilton Hotel in Washington DC, in 1981, the main entrance of hotels is being avoided for the highest ranked US politicians. It's not too often you come to greet the Vice President of the USA, with wife, at the receiving bay of a hotel. That place has never been so impeccably clean and nicely painted. Not too long before his tour of the

Middle East, Dick Cheney had had heart problems. We had strict instructions not to put any alcohol in his suite. In normal cases there would have been a full bar, but this time it was an array of fresh juices. Relatively late in the evening, the day of arrival, I was having a chat in the bar of the hotel with some guests, when a red-faced gentleman came rushing in. "I need a bottle of whiskey"! The Vice President had just returned from his talks with King Abdullah, and he was evidently thirsty. It was his secretary standing in the bar with an urgent request. With only juices as liquid in the suite, I realized the importance of the secretary's mission. Fast I went behind the bar counter and grabbed a bottle of Glenfiddich. "On the house," I said, pleased to help during an emergency. Anything for a VVIP! George Tenet, Director of the CIA and Paul Bremer, who led the Coalition Provisional Authority (CPA) following the 2003 invasion of Iraq, were two visiting US dignitaries who also caused much extra attention in regards to security from the US and Jordanian authorities.

There are occasions when you have the pleasure of hosting a VVIP from your own corporate HQ. At the beginning of 1998, Starwood acquired ITT, including the Sheraton hotels. This acquisition put an end to the hostile bid for ITT by Hilton Hotels

Corp. It was a strong battle between Rand Araskog, CEO of ITT, and Stephen Bollenbach, CEO of Hilton. Starwood was the white knight and one of the world's biggest hotel companies was created. 650 hotels in 70 countries with combined revenues of more than $10 billion and well-known brands including Sheraton, Westin, CIGA, Four Points, Luxury Collection and Caesars.

Starwood's CEO, Barry Sternlicht, took a vacation tour with his wife and kids to Europe and the Middle East, including Sheraton Soma Bay, during the Christmas holidays in 1999. Sami Zoghbi, then President Starwood Africa and Middle East, didn't take any risk in not providing the CEO world-class service. Information about food likings/dislikings of the family members was obtained and the whole show was set in motion. Overall, we were pretty pumped up, fully focused, choosing and selecting who would serve the family, who would clean the rooms/suites, who would monitor their every move.

A private jet was hired, to follow the route of the one of Sternlicht. In the "Zoghbi Jet" was Ludwig Simpson, Zoghbi's friend, and F&B consultant, together with Nicola, the Executive Chef of Sheraton Heliopolis and a German pastry chef, the best Starwood could offer in the Middle East. The plane was also stocked with food and beverage items, to the liking of the Sternlicht family, normally not being available in Egyptian hotels - what a spectacle! We planned the visit as if it would be a military exercise. Each department had detailed marching orders and strict lines of communication were established. It started already at the airport. We placed our F&B manager with service staff on the tarmac, greeting the family with fresh juices and canapés. Limo, off to Soma Bay. Two nights at the Sheraton kept us all alert. The visit can best be described as a combination of a state visit and a circus.

Barry Sternlicht was very nice and "down to earth" and Zoghbi didn't chase me, a good way of showing trust. We left the family alone and tried to act as if everything was normal. When Barry wanted to play tennis, we made sure that Mark, in charge of the resort's sport activities, beat him properly. This was the only tennis facility in the entire country that provided Gatorade, Barry's sports drink of choice. We pretty much worked around the clock with amateurish surveillance techniques, we followed him and communicated with each other about the family member's whereabouts. Mobiles were ringing between us regularly to keep us all up to date.

I was obviously around to check that the dinner was OK in L'Emporio, our Italian restaurant, on Christmas Eve, whilst our own kids were eagerly waiting to open the presents under the Christmas tree in our living-in accommodation. A "normal" Christmas Eve for a GM. To my knowledge, we only got Barry upset once. The pastry chef had to show his skills, so when ice cream was ordered as dessert for lunch it took close to 30 minutes, then a creation of ice cream, cherries, strawberry coulis, umbrellas, and whatever other decoration that could be found in the kitchen was presented. Even I could have produced two scoops of ice cream in two minutes and there wouldn't have been any smoke coming out of Barry's ears.

The famous Gatorade, that could soon be found in every corner of the resort, was transported, together with other food and beverage items, in a big steel box. The next stop for family Sternlicht was Sheraton Sharm El Sheik and the "Zoghbi Jet" took off with the famous box forgotten in Soma Bay. Crisis! Driver, van, box to Sharm El Sheik. The drive from Soma Bay to Sharm is about 13 hours, no bridge over / tunnel under the Red Sea. You have to drive along the coast to the Suez tunnel, cross, and then down the Sinai coast on the other side. A mega drive for a steel box. The driver left at 5 pm and arrived at Sharm at around 6 am the following day.

A more sensitive issue arose at the airport prior to take off. The luggage of family Sternlicht left the hotel in a separate van to the airport to be loaded onto the plane. Under normal circumstances this is a fast process. However, it's a very slow process when luggage is being scanned and corals are being found. A definite no-no to bring along from Egypt, and illegal, which the Sternlicht family was not aware of. I got a call from Moustafa, our Security Manager, for once not as cool as he was normally. We didn't want anything to become awkward for family Sternlicht at the airport. The corals were taken out of the luggage, and I asked Moustafa to pay whatever needed to be paid to whoever needed to be paid in order to make the problem go away. Barry was never told, and it must have been "a bit of a surprise" not finding the treasure when unpacking.

Is a corporate executive really more important than a paying guest? On occasions, yes. A common thesis is: if you cannot provide top service to a corporate executive, can you do it to your "normal guests?" In retrospect, did we overdo it? Maybe so.

The Sternlicht family obviously got much more attention than our other guests, though I do not think the actual service they received was much superior. I would most probably set the same preparation in motion had I been a GM today. Regardless, it was very nice to have Sheraton Soma Bay receiving a special mention from Barry Sternlicht in a speech at the next Starwood worldwide conference.

The host hotel for the top players of the Johnnie Walker Classic Golf Tournament in the spring of 2007. The tournament took place at the Blue Canyon Golf Club in Phuket. This is, for a golf nerd like me, as good as it gets in hosting a VIP Group. I cannot resist to name drop once more: Ernie Els, Adam Scott, Colin Montgomerie, Retief Goosen, Miguel Angel Jimenez, Paul Casey, Ian Woosnam, Sam Torrance, Mike Weir, many of them accompanied by their wife. Breakfast with Ernie Els, being served Johnnie Walker by Sam Torrance, gala dinner on the beach, rubbing shoulders with all of them, these are unforgettable memories.

What I learned from this event, and what we did very well, was to take full advantage of our cooperation and strong relationship with IMG, the tournament organizer. We secured the optimal hospitality area at Blue Canyon, a hotel suite with a balcony overlooking the 18th green. We catered first-class food and drinks from the Sheraton for four days. We joined forces with Virgin Australia and invited executives of the most important Australian tour operators. Free flight, free accommodation, top F&B, fantastic golf tournament. I can confirm that the invited VIPs were more than happy and our relationship with key accounts in a key feeder market was further strengthened.

Dress Code

There is a saying that as a host, you should never be better, or more formally, dressed than your guests. Maybe this works for a private dinner party, but not always for a GM of a hotel. I was the old-fashioned type, a bit of a snob. For me it was very important to be nicely dressed, to be perfectly dressed. I enjoyed putting on a well-tailored suit and felt comfortable knowing that everything was matching, the polished shoes, socks, belt, tie, and shirt. A nice way to start the day in a hotel with a lot of business travelers. I remember very well a former Sheraton colleague who once said: "Guests walking in a hotel corridor should see that it is the GM coming towards them, even if it is 50 meters away". Obviously, the dress code has changed over the years, and a tie has become a rare commodity amongst hotel GMs. Agreed, you can be properly dressed, without a tie. Beginning '90s in the Algarve, I, as Resident Manager, the GM, and all male department heads were dressed in a shirt and tie. Tie in a resort! This was the norm in those days, which luckily has changed, though it took some years.

Maybe I even went too far during my days as GM of the Sheraton Soma Bay. During daytime I wore bermuda shorts. Shorts with a nice short-sleeve button-down shirt and a pair of slick suede shoes. It looked smart. Dressed as described, I once welcomed Ulrich Eckhardt, then President of the Middle East, Africa & Indian Ocean for Kempinski Hotels. He took a second look at how I was dressed and, while standing in the lobby, he picked up his mobile phone and called what must have been his corporate HR executive. He instructed that, as of immediately, all GMs in his resorts should wear shorts. I felt like a real trendsetter.

My point is simple, the way the GM is dressed sets the standard for all non-uniformed staff members in the hotel. I'm sorry to say, but in this respect, I have seen some not-too-elegant role models.

As important is the dress code and behavior of the guests. For dinner at the Sheraton Soma Bay, we insisted on long trousers for men, which I think, in retrospect, might not have been necessary. At the end of the day, it does not matter how the guests are dressed when you see one "gentleman" attacking the leg of lamb, nicely displayed on the open kitchen counter. He grabs the leg of lamb with both hands and then takes a mega bite before putting it back on the counter. With, or without long trousers, hardly the way to behave in a 5-star resort. I have also seen examples of female guests showing a bit too much body for dinner in their see-throw outfits.

Competition

Get to know your competition. Get to know all their offerings and facilities. How can you otherwise stay ahead of the competition?

There are many easily available sources of information. Talk to mutual clients, check social media and reviews on booking platforms, dining experiences of friends, visit yourself. Be curious and learn from the competition.

Don't become complacent because your hotel has been no.1 in the compset for a long period of time. If you fall behind once, it can be a very steep mountain to climb to re-conquer the first place. On numerous occasions, I have also felt a superiority complex amongst hoteliers working for big international hotel companies (including myself as a fresh hotelier). The notion that an independent hotel cannot be operated as professionally as a hotel of "the Big Boys" is not uncommon, and so completely wrong.

As a GM, get to know your counterparts. There are numerous reasons for this, e.g., splitting big conferences/incentive groups, collaboration in destination marketing, support in eventual crises. In addition, hoteliers are normally very nice people to socialize with. What's interesting, especially when the competition is doing good business, is that GMs quite often tend to talk too much, i.e., giving away important, and too much information.

In Amman, we had an outstanding relationship and collaboration amongst the GMs of the 5-star hotels: Sheraton, Four Seasons, Grand Hyatt, Marriott, InterContinental and Le Royal. The best example of our working relation occurred shortly after the invasion of Iraq in March of 2003. Amman, together with Kuwait, became the gateways to Bagdad. Iraq suddenly was "the new Klondike", hence the hotel business was booming. For Sheraton, as well as for all major hotels, the US Embassy was a solid key account. Representatives of the US Embassy paid a visit to all 5-star hotels with some good news, we should expect a lot of business to be booked by the Embassy. The bad news was that they requested us to maximum charge the "per diem", which was an amount per night for accommodation, not to be exceeded, for state employees. Interesting that the USA was trying to influence the free market powers in Jordan. Zoom meetings did not exist in those days, but it was sufficient with a few telephone calls. This issue was solved within an hour. By no means a cartel, however we all agreed that the free market in Jordan was there to stay, without interference from the forces of the USA. We all charged as per the market conditions. The representatives of the US Embassy were not happy at all, the owners of the hotels were very happy.

On a regular basis, the GMs of the 5-star hotels met for a nice luncheon. It got better and better each time, as everyone wanted to beat the previous lunch. One of the most memorable meals took place during our famous camping trip in Wadi Rum, the beautiful desert with sandstone and granite rock formations. During the pre-dinner "drinks and snacks", Joseph Krahl, the GM of Grand Hyatt, exclaimed: "This must be the first time sushi, foie gras, and Dom Perignon is served in Wadi Rum!" We did enjoy some great culinary moments together.

Change of Guard

It's not for your own ego that you must leave a destination in style and with "the flag on top". The local community, and repeat guests, will talk about you as an individual and the hotel that you have represented. You should not forget that the image, and last impression, that you leave behind is also important to the owners, and the corporate office if you work for a management company. And owners also talk to each other. It's always of high importance that you have a smooth exit with a professional handover to your successor. Looking back on all the handovers that I have been involved with, as an outgoing or incoming GM, I think that there is too much emphasis on operational issues. I took over Sheraton Grande Laguna Phuket without handover from my predecessor. Same thing with two resorts in the Maldives, even though only for one month. Shortly thereafter a 1,100-room hotel in Hong Kong. What I am saying is, a hotel operation is a hotel operation and if you have a bit of experience, you will fast get a grip of the daily operation. To me, "less is more". It's not preferable to start fresh and be biased based on an overload of information from your predecessor. I would rather see the incoming and outgoing GMs spending time doing joint sales calls and the new GM to be introduced to key people in the local community, including fellow GMs at the competition.

Too many times have I heard a new GM having negative comments about the predecessor. Even the spouse gossiping in get-togethers. Just don't do it! It does not matter what has been done, or what you think, it reflects badly on you. Roll up your sleeves and get to work.

For an emotional person like me, the toughest part is the goodbye to all colleagues. This is the moment that I dread because you have experienced so much together, and you have achieved so much together, and suddenly it's gone. On the bright side, it's fantastic to start a new adventure.

As a family, we have made a few "nostalgia trips" to previous destinations, and the experience of meeting up with colleagues and friends of the past is wonderful!

What we seem to never learn

There are a few things in this industry that really upset me, one more stupid than the other. Let's start with breakfast service in a resort. This is the scenario; you know that all room rates include breakfast, and you are having a nice vacation in a resort by the sea. Every morning, arriving for breakfast, guests stay in line for 5-10 minutes before being seated. The reason being that the "breakfast host/ess" insists on asking for, and making a note of, your name and room number. All this time-consuming work, to the annoyance of already morning grumpy guests. Is this a procedure to safeguard against unwanted non-hotel guests having a free morning meal? If so, so be it, let them have it, it will happen "once in a blue moon". In addition, often the name list with room numbers is visible to all guests, hardly what the far more important safety and security policy prescribes.

Is it so hard to install a main light switch by the bed? If this is done, it is probably connected in a way that you oversleep because there is no electricity whatsoever in the room, hence your mobile phone with the wakeup call has not been charged. When doing a mock-up room, hours and hours are spent on design details, but often not enough attention is paid to lighting. Even worse in a suite. The first 10 minutes are spent running around, pushing buttons, and figuring out how the lighting system works. Put life in perspective, it's more than 50 years since we put a man on the moon. A common-sense lighting system in a hotel room/suite should be an easy fix.

Now, to many, the most annoying experience: bathroom amenities. Here we go: body lotion, shampoo, hair conditioner and shower gel—these are the four most common small bottles by the sink. Often of good quality with a nice fragrance. The issue is that five times out of ten, minimum, the text on these bottles is extremely small. If you're not a teenager with top eyesight, but in need of reading glasses, it is mission impossible to figure out what is what. It's not too often that you bring your glasses to the bathroom. You can hopefully figure out how to find the soap, most often liquid these days. After a shower comes the big quiz, the difference between hair conditioner and body lotion. I always use body lotion as an "aftershave," and without glasses, it's a 50/50. I have sometimes been too lazy to get my glasses and therefore rubbed my face with hair conditioner. Not very pleasant. Please, make the text BIG on these small, nice bottles!

I nearly forgot the blackout curtains, or lack of such. I do not think that I am exaggerating if I say that a minimum of 25% of the world's hotel rooms have curtains that do not completely cover the windows. It simply means that, due to streetlight in the evening or daylight in the morning, you will miss out on well-deserved sleep due to this annoying thin streak, or streaks, of light. Why do we pay for hotel accommodation? To sleep!

One more. Especially in Asia, there is a tendency in 5-star hotels to starch napkins, stiff like carbon. Impossible to be used for what it's supposed to be used for and when placed on your lap, it will take max 15 seconds before you have to pick it up from the floor. In addition to guest satisfaction, there are potential savings here. Stop starching napkins!

What I have learned

Surprise. In contrast to a common perception, life as a hotelier is often more demanding in a resort than in a business hotel. The recommended scenario is to experience both.

The Competition.

- **To beat the competition** you need to know their services and facilities in detail. Be curious and learn from the competition.

- **Laser focus, and deliver, on the basics** and you will beat the competition.

First, and last impression can make it or break it.

P&L. Department Heads are not only responsible for service delivery. They have to know the financial impact of all initiatives and actions in place to deliver services. A well-prepared and executed monthly P&L meeting is of the highest priority.

The yearly budget to be supported by a very solid strategy.

Meetings. Make sure to time internal meetings not to conflict with the operations. Make them short and efficient. Certain meetings can benefit from the rotation of the chairmanship.

Complacency – Watch out! In good days, make sure to look ahead and plan for future success, do not get stuck in past glory.

Look ahead. Not only for tomorrow and next week. What are the priorities for next month, next quarter......

Visibility is a cornerstone to being a successful GM. A GM cannot run the hotel from the office. Get to know the operation by being around. Get to know your associates, obtain direct feedback from your guests.

Cleanliness. The reason for choosing your hotel might be location, pricing, or your loyalty program. One thing is for sure, the guest will never come back if the cleanliness is not of the highest standard.

SOPs. Allow your associates to be flexible. SOPs should be the guidelines, though common sense should always prevail. Safety and security and handling of money are the areas where implementation has to be rigid. SOP for eventual crisis of utmost importance.

Complaints. A system to be in place to communicate all complaints timely to the GM, who should be actively involved in resolving, learning from, and following up on complaints. Admit mistakes, be honest and be trustworthy. In many cases, it can be useful to take advantage of the telephone.

VIPs should be given the extra attention that they deserve, without overdoing it.

Change of guard. Introduction of the incoming GM to clients and key people in the local community to be the focus. In terms of operations, less is often more.

Technology should ideally implemented to the benefit of the guests, not exclusively to facilitate more efficient operation for the hotel associates. Make sure to be on top of, and control, the implementation of technology. Closely follow the evolution of Artificial Intelligence (AI) and how the overall hotel operation can benefit from AI.

Sustainable, eco-friendly hotel environment has to be a top priority. The core elements revolve around reducing waste, saving energy, and cutting down on water usage.

The Owner is always the most important stakeholder, also when you are engaged by a management company. In this case, it's important to find a balance in the relation with both "higher powers," sometimes with contradicting views. The GM's diplomatic skills will sometimes be put to the test.

Enjoy and have fun. You should be pleased to have chosen such a great profession. The day-to-day operation should be fun – enjoy it!

OWNER RELATIONS

Regardless if you work directly for an owner or represent a management/operating company, the relationship you establish as a GM with the owner will decide your destiny.

When I refer to owner, it can be the person who owns the hotel, or a person being a part-owner and representing the investors. It can also be an asset manager, representing the owner/s.

The owner is in it to make money. Most often, the relationship with the owner is directly correlated with the financial results of the hotel. On good days, accumulate as much "goodwill" as possible, it's needed for worse days to come, because they will come!

Trust must be established. Trust is the key; the owner must feel confident that you are a "person of your word" and that there is no double agenda on the horizon. Trust can only be established if transparency exists. This is a two-way street, by doing your part you are more than halfway to establishing a solid ground for a smooth and beneficial working relation.

You will usually have formal meetings with the owner. It could be monthly P&L meetings or board meetings. You must be extremely well prepared for these meetings and be in total control of the finances, and other issues, of the hotel. This is the formal part of the relationship. Sometimes, even more important is the informal part. A coffee at the deli, a drink in the bar, a lunch outside the hotel or a round of golf. Invest time to get to know the owner, and/or the representative, and establish a relationship that reaches outside the life of the hotel. Sometimes, pick up the phone, not necessarily to discuss a specific issue relating to the hotel, but just to "catch up".

Of utmost importance, never forget that the owner knows everything that goes on in the hotel. Even if this is not always the case, assume that it is! When you arrive as GM, everyone realizes that it is for a limited period, and most people around you have been at the hotel for years, and they will stay on for years to come. Common sense tells you that the strongest loyalty is towards the owner, having well-established contacts, and friends, in the hotel.

As an example, I remember Bill Heinecke, founder, and at the time CEO of Minor Hotels, at the beginning of my time as GM of Anantara Riverside in Bangkok, once said something like: "I do not need a Resident Manager, I have Khun Pailin (the PA to the GM since many years – my remark), she can run the show and she lets me know what's going on. I haven't heard anything negative about you."

Confidentially belongs within the concept of trust. Representing an operating company, you will occasionally be trusted with confidential information and sometimes the owner will ask you to treat certain information confidentially.

Stay away from the temptation to communicate any confidential information, it could cost you dearly, as per the "horror story" to follow.

"There is a rat in the room"

During my days in Egypt, at the Sheraton Soma Bay, 1999-2002, there was usually a quarterly meeting in Cairo for all GMs in Egypt. The meeting took place in the office of Sami Zoghbi, President Starwood Africa and Middle East. We all enjoyed each other's company, and Cairo, as messy as it is, was still a nice break from the desert by the Red Sea.

This time, we were gathered in the meeting room in the basement of the office. No windows, and as soon as Mr. Zoghbi lit a fat cigar, then all smokers, including myself, lit the cigarettes. What a smog, what an environment. I cannot remember the exact number of participants, 8-10. Each GM gives a brief rundown of the business in a relatively casual atmosphere. Mr. Zoghbi, as usual, is very outspoken about what he thinks about the respective hotel, and its owner. In the evening of the meeting, we were a few that went out for dinner in Cairo. During pre-dinner drinks, one of us receives a call from Jessie, Mr. Zoghbi's PA. Strict instructions, all participants of the day's meeting to be back in the office the following morning. You can imagine the speculations during dinner. We were not called to receive roses, that's for sure.

11.00 am the following day, we are all back in the dungeon. There was a strange feeling in the room, a feeling of curiosity and a nervous feeling. Mr. Zoghbi starts with something along the lines of: "Do we agree that what we say in this room is confidential, and should be kept confidential?" You could hear a "yes" echoing. Then came the famous: "There is a rat in the room"! We were then told that a harsh comment during yesterday's meeting, expressed by Mr. Zoghbi, regarding an owner had the same day been communicated to the owner in question. A very awkward silence in the room, until someone tried to save the situation. "Sami, could it not be a misunderstanding?"

He was immediately interrupted by Mr. Zoghbi, "No, there is a rat in the room!" If possible, an even more awkward atmosphere. He then explained that there would be severe repercussions for "the rat." I do not know how the information traveled to the owner in question, though it did not take too long before we all figured out who "the rat" was. He did not stay on very long with Sheraton.

Stay away from the temptation to communicate any confidential information, it could cost you dearly.

Figures

Whenever it is, wherever you are, know your figures!

I have mentioned Bill Heinecke, the founder of Minor Hotels. He knows his figures, and if not, he makes sure to have access to them. When I was Area GM for the Anantara hotels in South Thailand, we opened a stunning resort, Anantara Layan in Phuket. The construction of the beautiful, US$ 10-12 million, villas overlooking the Andaman Sea was not completed at the time of opening the resort. It was obviously of interest and concern to Mr. Heinecke. One Saturday we took an SUV around the development to check the status of the construction. It was Bill Heinecke, with his wife, Andy Kunz, the GM and behind the wheel, me.

After an hour's tour, Mr. Heinecke asked if Andy and I would like to join for a quick lunch. I still regret that I accepted the invitation, even though it became a good lesson learned. For lunch Mr. Heinecke brought two things close to his heart, his charming wife Kathy, and his airline pilot case with key figures of all Minor hotels, not as charming. I have always been good with figures, i.e., good at analyzing figures, however lousy at remembering figures. Cross-examination of Andy and myself. We were totally taken by surprise, expecting a nice casual lunch. He started off by asking about the capture rate of the spa, and from thereon, it went downhill. Kathy soon realized how humiliated we were and left for another table after 30 minutes.

Einstein has said that one shouldn't overload the brain with information that is easily obtainable. Well said, however, in this situation there was only one person that had access to the information, it was not me and it was not Andy. Lesson learned; always have your figures available when you know that higher powers, most importantly the owner, is in the neighborhood.

I might have portrayed Bill Heinecke in a bad light. It should be noted that he is a person that I have the highest respect for, and I truly admire his passion for his people and his hotels.

Direct line to the Owner

I have earlier touched on my first experience working directly with an owner, as GM of the 1,100-room Regal Airport Hotel in Hong Kong. Regal Hotels International is one of the largest hotel groups in Hong Kong and is listed on the Hong Kong Stock Exchange. The company is controlled by its chairman and managing director, Mr. Lo Yuk Sui. After 28 years with Sheraton/Starwood it was tough to adapt to the fact that I was working directly with the owner of a hotel. With Starwood you were captain of your ship, with support from your boss when needed. You were basically running your own show, therefore a fulfilling working environment. I very quickly realized that my working life was about to change dramatically.

During one of the first morning meetings (which I timewise cut in half) I found out that the housekeeping department was short of staff and outside service was engaged to support. I acted as I would normally do and instructed the HR responsible to immediately start the hiring process of ten room maids. "I need approval from the corporate office," was the reply. I was not in the mood to listen and repeated my instructions, maybe a bit louder. Then the paperwork started with forms to be completed and submitted to the corporate office. A tough start, and tough to swallow.

Next surprise, I would say shock, was the monthly reporting. Starwood had a lean monthly report that was working very well. It gave a clear picture of the business and was not too time-consuming. The monthly report for Regal Hotels was seldom below three hundred pages, 300 pages! For the first monthly report, January 2011, I called BY, the CEO, and told her that due to the recent firing of the Director of Finance we had issues in putting together a report as per the normal format. No "300-pager" and no monthly presentation, which could last up to a full day. I got away with it the first month, but realized that going forward, I just had to fall in line. It is a challenge to acclimatize to a business environment where all decisions of importance are taken at the corporate level. In addition, when the monthly report is presented, you are only faced with criticism, hardly ever did we receive a positive comment or a suggestion for improvement.

Anyway, I got along well with BY, my boss. To my knowledge, the only time she questioned my judgment, and rightly so, was after my "confrontation" with the chairman's daughter. In Hong Kong, Alex Haeusler, Resident Manager, and I, both lived in, hence it was rare that not one of us was present in the hotel. However, one Friday evening, we were both absent and the hotel was visited by the chairman's daughter. I had a phone call whilst enjoying a nice dinner at my favorite Argentinian steak house in Lan Kwai Fong in central Hong Kong. I left the noisy restaurant to be able to speak in relative peace in the street. Constructive feedback from the owner is fine and appreciated, though depending on how it is communicated. The daughter was upset because the food in the hotel was not to her satisfaction. I do not know if it was her food, or the food for her dogs. She gave me a good lesson on how to operate a hotel. After a while I had enough and simply told her: "I was a GM when you were still in diapers!" Not a smart comment if you want to strengthen the relationship with the owner. She hung up, not me.

Next time as a "direct-line GM" was in Sweden, after having given up on my Hong Kong adventure. I was interim GM in two hotels in south Sweden, combined during a period of eight months. I am grateful to Uwe Loeffler, the founder, and CEO of Ligula Hotels, for having left me alone, "doing my thing". He realized fast that I would give him a call if support was needed. However, when you work under these circumstances, it's important that you regularly keep the owner in the loop. The "trust factor" is huge.

Next experience, working direct for the owner, was Minor Hotels in Thailand, my last two years in operation, 2013 -2015. Quite a change from Regal Hotels, a positive such. On a day-to-day basis, you were quite free to run your hotel as per your liking if you delivered top service and delivered top dollars. Minor is extremely bottom-line oriented and let me quote myself: "The owner is in it to make money. Most often, the relationship with the owner is directly correlated with the financial results of the hotel." If you do not make the forecast or budget for the month, you better have the answers – money talks!

Management Agreement

It's a totally different working environment when you represent a management company towards an owner of a hotel. All the major international hotel companies are today "asset light", i.e., they generate income through fees from management agreements and franchise agreements. To get it all in perspective, let's start with the management agreement.

The most common agreement, except in the USA, is for the operator to charge a percentage fee on the topline revenue and an incentive fee of the adjusted GOP, often a percentage scale based on performance. In the USA, the incentive fee is based on achieving the owner's expected ROI, hence the incentive fee is usually more difficult to achieve. On rare occasions, the operator would guarantee the hotel owner a profit. The reason for this could be that the location of the hotel would be very sought after.

A travel magazine wrote: "A press release from Accor, then it must be a new brand." Why all these new brands? Very simply put, international hotel companies will otherwise run out of brands that would enable them to sign new management agreements. Clauses normally stipulate that two hotels with the same brand cannot be located within a certain radius of each other. The best example is the "lifestyle brands." There is no other reason for all new brands in this category. The challenge for the management companies is to differentiate the brands, and more importantly, for the potential owner to understand the differentiation, and even more importantly, for the potential guest to understand what the brands stand for. I know that I am side tracking, and I am not going to dive into the discussion of branding of hotels. However, branding is supposed to create a distinct identity. To me, as a hotel guest, the branding of hotels is just a big "ratatouille," with empty phrases often defining and describing the same thing. If not done, a great subject for hotel school students could be a thorough analysis of what different brands stand for, and the perception of the guests.

I once had an owner who said: "General Managers are only concerned about the GOP, nothing else." I politely told him that we cannot affect what's below the GOP line, however if we are informed about the owner's financial obligations, we would know what to aim for. As of that day, I had a very stretched financial "owner target". As a rule, it is important to know what financial obligations the owner has, and this is something you should inquire about, though maybe not your first day at work. What's also of interest is what the management company has "promised" the owner. The figures that the owner believed in (?) at the time of signing the agreement. When figures do not materialize, the owner is not interested in being referred to various waivers in some feasibility study, they will always come back to the financial results that once have been communicated as "achievable" by the management company.

As GM, you should know the most important paragraphs of the management agreement and where to find whatever information you need. It's not easy to read parts of some management agreements. There can be sentences of ½ an A4 page with 27 commas and 12 brackets. It will definitely keep your brain cells active.

In Egypt, "Mr. Soma Bay," Dr. Farid Saad, "a Gentleman and a half," once gave me a good indication of how some owners deal with the content of the management agreement. The Sheraton Soma Bay was not even one year old when I arrived, and shortly thereafter, I realized that the fabric on the chairs and sofas in the lobby had already started to wear off. I reviewed the management agreement, and I found ammunition to approach Dr. Farid. It stipulated that the owner should provide 10% spare of fabrics for all furniture. I asked Dr. Farid where the spares were to be found, and politely referred to the management agreement. A fast, and short, answer: "I have never read the management agreement", nothing further to discuss. In general, I would say that you should avoid referring to the management agreement, it becomes a "red flag" to the owner and should be the last option to solve an eventual disagreement.

An interesting conflict, and a legal case, regarding management agreement, arose in Thailand, between Minor International as the owner and Marriott Hotels as the operator. Minor is suing Marriott for alleged non-performance of the JW Marriott Resort & Spa in Phuket, which it fully owns. Short, it relates to the Marriott Bonvoy loyalty program and the rates offered via this program. Also, the fact that Marriott operates another 10 hotels on the island, competing with the Minor owned. This could also be an interesting case for hotel school students to analyze.

Let's briefly touch on the difference between a management agreement and a franchise agreement. As a hotel owner, you might want to operate the hotel yourself, but as a franchisee, take advantage of the brand of an international hotel chain. The advantages are mainly the brand recognition, to be included in the reservation system and the loyalty program. Your hotel would have to adhere to certain, relatively strict, standards and will be charged a variety of franchise fees. There are also "3rd part companies" (TPMCs) that specialize in operating franchised hotels on behalf of the owners. This is far more common in the USA than in the rest of the world.

Dotted line to the Owner

As a GM in a hotel guided by a management agreement, your direct reporting line to the operating company is clear, however, as important is your reporting line to the owner, let's call it the "dotted reporting line". The relation can be complicated when you, as discussed earlier, must balance the opinion of the owner and the instructions of the operator. Important also is the trust between the GM and the executives of the management company. The GM is *the person* representing the brand towards the owner. However, it's not always that all representatives of the corporate office are highly regarded.

In the beginning of my Sheraton life, the corporate office covering Europe was in Denham, outside London. SMC Denham, Sheraton Management Corporation Denham, or as it used to be called by some, Seagull Management Corporation – "They fly in, they shit on you, and fly out again."

At all times, think like an owner and consider the big decisions involving cost as if you were an owner and it was your money - would you do it? Don't try to sell something to an owner unless you believe in it yourself, e.g., a newly built hotel in Thailand having to order brand standard beds from USA, cost wise it does not make sense. Get the corporate "brand gurus" to reconsider and find a local manufacturer that can be approved and make the brand-standard beds locally. It makes good business sense, and the owner will recognize the effort to save money.

"Behind every great owner there's a great woman". I was once on the edge of accepting an interesting GM assignment in Singapore. An opening, which I like, with a well-established international brand. I was "ticked off" by the operating company and the lunch with the chairman and some board members was very positive. All good, until I met the chairman's wife and I realized who was in charge. In principle, not a problem, however I didn't appreciate her approach - "I decide, you run". I would not have enjoyed a dotted line to this lady.

It's always beneficial to find out who is the true decision maker within the organization of the owner. In Soma Bay, it was Dr. Farid who called the shots of the owners. However, his wife Nevine was a strong character with strong opinions, especially related to certain associates. It took two weeks after my arrival, then I had the pleasure of Madame paying a visit to my office. I had inherited two assistant F&B managers, and she insisted that one of them, whom she disliked, had to go. It does not matter what I thought about the person in question, there was no way, as GM, that you could agree and obey to such a request, even though Mme. Nevine "represented" the owners. I responded with a diplomatic: "Let me evaluate". Much later Mme. Nevine complained about the quality of our pizza. Not once, repeatedly. I knew that her opinion was not common, but I could not "silence" her. Franz Kielnhofer, Executive Assistant Manager, and I initiated a "pizza survey" and during the period of one week had one hundred guests complete this "sophisticated" questionnaire that luckily resulted in our advantage, 94% excellent. No further discussion about pizza quality after having presented the result to Mme Nevine. Sometimes you must go to the extreme to get an "owner representative" off your back.

Dr. Farid had his office in Cairo but spent close to every weekend in the resort. In a Muslim country, which means Friday and Saturday. In theory these were my two days off. However, living-in, and running high occupancy over the weekends, it was not too much of a difference, except for spending as much time as possible with Helle and the kids. Dr. Farid quite often sends me a fax before leaving his office on Thursday afternoons. It could be remarks relating to the operation, questions concerning sales and marketing, capex issues, anything that he wanted to discuss over the weekend. As soon as I saw a "Thursday fax", I knew that a chunk of the weekend was gone. He didn't send me the fax to be mean, he rather did it for me to be prepared. In the best case we sorted everything out during a round of golf. The conclusion here is that regardless of where and when the owner prefers to meet up with you, be there and be well prepared.

An important rule is to keep the owner in the loop. With a few exceptions, the owner wants to know what's going on; hiring and firing, food promotions, sales trips and so on. Once again, be transparent, there is nothing to hide. During a pre-opening, I experienced a GM who did not inform the owner about the hotel's inauguration party. The party was canceled (at the time already 300 guests had been invited) and not long thereafter also the GM.

The best sign of a well-established relationship with the owner I experienced in Oslo. With few exceptions, all hotels in Oslo had a labor dispute and the negotiations with the union stalled. The employer's organization called for a lock-out, and no unionized staff members, representing maybe 95 % in our case, were allowed in their workplace. There were demonstrations outside the hotel, and a total mess for a couple of days. Impossible for guests to enter the hotel. This was a situation that became the ultimate test of our owner relations. The issue was that, on day two, we had the Air France crew arriving. I am sure we could have referred to "force majeure", however bearing in mind the importance of Air France to Sheraton worldwide, we desperately wanted to find a solution. The owner came to our rescue. Preben Mehren, our key contact person representing the owning company, came up with the solution. Preben's home, at Voksenkollen, with a stunning view overlooking Oslo, is hard to describe, just a dream. I can assure you that there is no Air France crew in the history of the airline, that ever has had a better accommodation, and a nicer dinner together. Not only did this episode further strengthen our relationship with the owner, but it also strengthened the relationship, and collaboration, between Sheraton Corporation and Air France.

As GM, I have dealt with several owners over the years, and I have an interesting observation. In statistical terms, it's not reliable at all, but worthwhile mentioning anyway. Two of the owner's representatives that I have appreciated the most have had a military background. The reason for my appreciation is that both had the same qualities, i.e., nice, calm, straightforward, knowledgeable, and transparent. If this is a pure coincidence, or relates to their background, I do not know. I am inclined to believe the latter.

Even though you have a budget stamped by the management company, it might not be the figures that are acceptable to the owner. Here we go, one budget for the corporate office and another one for the owner. This situation should not be allowed to happen and you, as GM, play a vital role, sometimes together with your boss, to make sure that you derive a budget that is acceptable for both parties. Needless to say, all criteria related to the bonus should also be crystal clear and signed off by the owner. As financials usually have the heaviest weight in the bonus calculation, there should be no room for interpretation.

I have mentioned Dr. Farid Saad, "Mr. Soma Bay". His brother Jimmy was living in the resort, and so did Helle and I, with the kids. Jimmy had an office in the lobby where he was promoting the sale of houses around the golf course in Soma Bay. This meant, not only I, but also the rest of the family saw a lot of Jimmy, like his brother, a real gentleman. In the absence of Dr. Farid, Jimmy functioned as the owner's representative, even if this was not his formal duty. Jimmy and I became quite close, and over time also the rest of the family. The saying is that intoxicated adults as well as kids tell the truth, and our kids told the truth without hesitation. Victor, 7 years old, had obviously heard his dad elaborating about the life as GM as well as the life of an owner, which came to light one day when Jimmy asked Victor: "Are you also going to become a hotel manager when you grow up?" Without blinking, the 7-year-old said: "No, I'll be an owner!" He already realized who was the most important.

Emilie, 5 years old, had not started her course in diplomacy the day Jimmy asked her: "Emilie, are we getting married when you grow up?" "Jimmy, when I am old enough to get married, you'll be dead!" First, and last, time Jimmy mentioned marriage to our daughter.

I had to deal with an interesting scenario relating to owners at the Sheraton Grande Laguna Phuket (2006-2010). Within the complex of the resort, we had 52 "Island Villas." No real villas, more like duplex suites, located in a separate part of the resort. The suites are in a rental pool under the management of the Sheraton. The owners can use their unit a certain number of weeks per year, excluding "blackout weeks" during high-demand periods. Legally, the set-up is a CJP (Condominium Juristic Person). The law states that foreigners may only own 49% of the unit area available. This was something new for me as a hotelier. The CJP and Condominium Act, sinking fund, common are fee, maintenance fee, rules and regulations. Most important, and most demanding, 52 owners to deal with. However, most owners did not raise their voices for one reason, there were no CJP on the island, with a similar set-up, generating as much return to the owners as Sheraton did. Money talks. However, the annual general meeting always brought on some interesting comments from some, usually the same, owners. The headache started when we were about to plan a well-needed renovation of the units. When to do it, how much can it cost, financing, design...? We froze the return to the owners for a long period, got a good interior designer on board, a "hard to deal with" contractor, made a mock-up unit (disaster), made a second mock-up unit, and went ahead with limited input from the owners. Within time, nearly, and within budget. This would have taken years had we gone the "democratic route" asking for input from 52 owners. One owner, representing a few owner friends, came to me with some suggestions. I was quoted to have said: "You want a Taj Mahal but pay for an IKEA renovation." We went ahead as planned and, when completed, received a lot of praise.

Sometimes it's worthwhile to take a risk, to act fast, go ahead and deal with the consequences afterwards.

My last assignments as GM were 2013-2015 with Minor Hotels. The first year in Bangkok as GM of Anantara Riverside and Area GM for the own Anantara branded assets in Thailand, from Chang Rai to Phuket. This was the first time I had other GMs reporting to me. A challenge and a good experience. An even better experience was the second year, when the area responsibility for the Anantara hotels was split geographically. I then oversaw south Thailand as an area, and I was GM of Anantara Phuket Villas. The hotels in south Thailand were a mix of owned and managed hotels. A new challenge, as I now had to deal with owners, but in a more senior position. Overall, the owners were satisfied with their GMs, though on occasions I had to intervene and use the best skills of diplomacy and decision-making. The aim was always to fix the issue at hand as smoothly as ever possible. I had area responsibility, and I was there to sort out any problem. I did not want anything to escalate upwards in the hierarchy. For one, my boss, the COO, was sometimes more difficult to handle than the owners.

It does not matter if you are GM or have an area responsibility, the basics relating to owner relationships are the same. Again, to me the key words are transparency and trust.

A Dissatisfied Owner

I have personally always had good relations with the representatives of the various owning companies during my many years with ITT Sheraton / Starwood, as well as when I worked directly for the Owners at Regal Hotels, Ligula Hotels and Minor Hotels. Despite this, it was an owner who changed the course of my life when I had to quit as GM of the Sheraton Grande Laguna Phuket, A Luxury Collection Resort. It's a long story, but in the context of owner relationship, it's "a good one" and worthwhile to share. There are some interesting learnings.

How did I mess it up and what can be learned from it?

I am not in a position to sort out the legal entities of the ownership of Sheraton Grande Laguna Phuket. Regardless, the hotel was under the umbrella of Laguna Resorts and Hotels, controlled by Mr. Ho Kwon Ping (usually referred to as "KP"), founder and Executive Chairman of Banyan Tree Holdings and Laguna Resorts and Hotels. A visionary who, amongst others, developed the entire Laguna Resort complex on the island of Phuket as well as Laguna Lang Co, a resort complex in Vietnam. KP is a living legend in Asia, not only in the world of hotel and travel, but within the entire business community.

A strike broke out in Laguna in February of

2009. My take is that the outcome of this strike was the main reason for KP to insist on me leaving as the GM of the Sheraton Grande Laguna Phuket, even though it took quite some time before it actually happened. Laguna was, and is, the biggest private employer on the island, with around 3,500 staff members at the time of the strike, the vast majority unionized. The hotels concerned were Laguna Beach Resort, the Dusit Thani Resort, the Sheraton Grande Laguna Phuket, the Banyan Tree, the Allamanda and the Laguna Holiday Club. In addition, the strike also involved the laundry service, the golf club, and some other services within Laguna. The dispute revolved around the lack of a bonus which usually appears in the pay of staff in January.

In my view, this strike would never have happened, had the Laguna executives adhered to what was agreed by them and the GMs of the hotels a couple of days prior to the strike, i.e., the agreed financial compensation and settlement for the Laguna employees to avoid a rumored future strike. Unfortunately, no minutes were taken at this meeting, and it was never referred to either. It didn't matter the moment the strike broke out. A "blaming game" was not of interest. However, had meeting minutes been taken and agreed actions followed by concerned parties, my future hotel life would have most probably looked different.

The strike meant that staff, with very few exceptions, did not show up for work, supplies could not reach the hotels as strikers blocked the entrances, the outside laundry facilities could not be used, and guests had to be escorted in and out from the hotels for security reasons. The union that started the strike had lost control of the situation by day three. The local police had washed their hands of the situation and did not make any attempt to clear the blockade, resulting in all-night parties, coyote dancers and alcohol, so any chance of negotiation to resolve the situation was out of the question.

Lyndon Ellis, the Resident Manager, and I, concluded that there was simply no way we could continue to operate the hotel under these conditions. The hotel was getting filthy, with only one restaurant operating on whatever was left in fridges and freezers (basically the same buffet for breakfast, lunch and dinner – not very impressive), non-existent outside laundry service and only a few staff members including management, all literary walking on their knees. We had no choice but to close the hotel and get all guests transported to other hotels on the island, which took place on day five of the strike. We were the only hotel in Laguna that took this drastic step as we were in a much tougher situation than our "sister hotels," mainly due to the high number of guests in our hotel. It was a 410-room hotel running 85% occupancy with nearly 100% double occupancy, i.e., close to 700 guests in-house when the strike started, with around 100 guests checking out during the strike. It was a cumbersome task, to say the least, to evacuate 600 guests under the circumstances we were faced with. We were acting for the good of our guests, for the good of our owner, and for the good of the Sheraton and Luxury Collection brands.

One can obviously not close a Luxury Collection Resort without having the consent of the owner, which I received over the phone from the owner's representative. It's still a mystery to me why I did not put it in writing. It can maybe be explained by my exhaustion at that point. The next step was to obtain approval from Sheraton, which went fast as we had the OK from the owner.

On day six, the strike was over, without any union negotiations, and we took two days to deep clean the hotel and get ready for guests to arrive. This was one day too many, as per the owner representative who did not understand the work we had at hand. However, I, and all of us, received outstanding support from my Sheraton boss, Wayne Buckingham. I called him in Bangkok on a Sunday, asking for his support and he was on the first flight to Phuket on Monday morning. This took place after the strike was over, however we had a lot to deal with, amongst others, various meetings with the staff. We also had some memorable meetings with the union leaders.

On my last working day, the local owner representative told me that the closing of the hotel had played a role in the owning company asking for a new GM (I couldn't resist asking). This, despite the fact that financially the hotel was consistently "the flavor of the month." I can only speculate (!) that, to cover his own rear, either he did not inform KP of his approval to close the hotel, or he just did not support me towards KP, who admittedly is a strong force. No one, apart from the limited number of Sheraton employees who stayed in the hotel during the strike, had a true picture of the difficulties that we were facing.

The strike in Laguna relates to issues that might not be discussed in hotel schools, though some are obvious.

You learn:

- That important decisions should be put in writing. One meeting leading up to the strike, and one telephone conversation during the strike, should have been properly recorded, and communicated to concerned parties.

- That you should NEVER scream over the phone when an owner representative confronts you. He didn't like the two-day post-strike closure for cleaning. I loudly disagreed.

- Who your friends are. One specific hotel increased the rate to benefit from our situation when evacuating a big number of guests to this hotel.

- To ask for help, which probably should be done more often.

- Who your boss truly is.

- To be very visible at times of "crisis." We put a desk in the lobby with the sign "Management," either manned by the Resident Manager or me. Many potential post-strike complaints were avoided by being accessible to the guests. We only had two guest complaints following the strike.

- That something must be fundamentally wrong when you find the chief engineer in the kitchen cooking for the dinner buffet.

- Who amongst your executive team "steps up to the plate" when most needed. They all did.

- That the relationship with an owning company should never be underestimated.

Sometimes, but very rarely, you get a bit of the upper hand towards the owner. In Amman, the ownership of the Sheraton Hotel was controlled by the Mouasher family, with the family head, Nadim Mouasher as the chairman. The family also controlled the ownership of the three Marriotts in Jordan (Amman, Dead Sea, and Petra). Mr. Nadim was always quite negative and vocal about the fact that his late brother had signed a management agreement with Sheraton and not Marriott (this was long before the Marriott acquisition of Starwood, including the Sheraton brand). I believe it was one month during the summer of 2003, when we realized that our GOP was higher than the three Marriott's combined. I politely reminded Mr. Nadim of this fact and that Sheraton was not all that bad and we did produce the numbers. Not to rub it in, but it felt good.

What I have learned

The strike in Laguna, Phuket was a lesson in itself with described take-aways.

Establish a good relationship with the owner. This is your lifeline. Work on it. It doesn't happen overnight. Be transparent and build trust.

Confidentiality. Never forget the true meaning of confidentiality and stick to it.

Keep the owner up to date with what's going on in the hotel. "No surprise is the best surprise".

Meetings. Make sure to be extremely well prepared for owner meetings. It is also important to initiate non-formal communication with the owner. These kinds of meetings can sometimes be more important than the formal ones.

Think like an owner when it relates to expenditure.

Take advantage of the owner's connections. It can generate a lot of business.

Know your figures. There is nothing more frustrating for an owner than a GM who is not on top of the figures. I still meet GMs who don't know the difference between % and %-points!

The Management Agreement (MA). If a MA,

know "your rights", but always try to solve any issues or disagreement without referring to the MA. This should be the last resort.

Bonus. Make sure not to miss out on this extra financial incentive. If a MA, have the owner to approve / sign off on the bonus criteria for you and all concerned executives.

Nothing is more important than the bottom line. There are many important KPIs. For the owner, none that beats the financial ones.

MANAGEMENT AND LEADERSHIP

Initially my intention was to avoid the subjects of management and leadership. Few topics in the business world have been honored with so much literature. Daily you see quotes about how to act, react and behave as a manager and a leader. It's difficult to contribute something new to this field. However, the more I thought about the managers/leaders I have worked with, in addition to my own experience, I couldn't resist a few thoughts.

What is What?

What is the difference between a manager and a leader? I found the below definition, which I think is spot on.

"Overall, the key difference is that a manager

will focus on planning, organizing, and coordinating resources to manage tasks and deliver results. A leader will inspire, motivate, and influence those around them which will drive people to achieve their goals and objectives whilst working towards the bigger picture." (Robert Half Talent Solutions, n.d.)

Obviously, you can be a good manager and not a good leader or vice versa. The challenge is to be a good manager AND a good leader, a combination which might not be common.

Management

Most importantly, the manager is responsible for delivering organizational goals, and they should be crystal clear to be understood by all stakeholders. Similarly, the strategies and action plans to reach the established goals should also be clear. It's the manager's responsibility to follow up and communicate the status towards agreed goals. Management skills can, to a large extent, be taught. I firmly believe that a "not-too-good" manager can be trained to become an efficient manager.

Leadership

I have read a limited amount of literature on leadership. The reason, maybe not logical, being that it is very hard to take on, and adapt to, all the suggestions about how to behave as a leader. My personal, very simple, thesis: **Be yourself and build relationships**. In the long run, "you are who you are." You perform in your daily leadership role the way you feel comfortable. Either you are a born leader (what a cliché) or not. You can pick up from literature how to act in certain situations towards certain types of co-workers, though be true to yourself. Without building close relationships with your team members, you will not succeed. Build relationships based on transparency and trust. For me this is the fundament as a leader. A leader then needs the ability to communicate the vision and strategies of the hotel. The way Jan Carlzon, CEO of SAS Airline from 1981 to 1994, in his book *"A Moment of Truth"*, describes a leader can very well be applied to a GM of a hotel. With "a moment of truth," Jan Carlzon means the few seconds or minutes a customer contact may last, but that reflects the "functionality" of the whole organization. *"A customer-driven company is one that recognizes that its only true asset is satisfied* *customers*. A leader of such a company can't be an isolated and autocratic decision-maker. Instead, he or she must be a visionary, a strategist, an informer, a teacher, and an inspirer." So true, though a tall order for many leaders, including hoteliers.

I have experienced many leadership styles, the two extremes being "Leadership by Fear" and "Teddy Bear Leadership". Both GMs successful in having subordinates working hard, however, I saw tears leaving the GM's office and I saw smiles leaving the GM's office. One leadership style evidently produces a happier working environment than the other. "Leadership by Fear" will never hold in the long run. Maybe also the case for "Teddy Bear Leadership."

How can you inspire co-workers if you don't know when and how to give praise? As Resident Manager, I once had a GM asking me: "Are you the type that needs praise?" Unfortunately, I was too proud, or not confident enough, to say "Yes". I would think that 99 % appreciate, and thrive on, well-deserved praise. I had a couple of bosses who could not spell praise, but you also grew accustomed to this kind of leadership. If you do not hear anything, all is OK – No news is good news. Silence is praise! When something is not to the liking of this leader, you would loudly, or very loudly, hear it. Probably it could be described as "tough leadership." I do contradict myself, but late in life, I appreciated "silent praise." For whatever reason, I felt more content to satisfy the "tough leader" than the "softer" one.

I must get off my chest what I consider to be the worst kind of leadership, which I unfortunately have experienced, the "Cowardly Leadership." This is the leader that face-to-face is the nicest person that you can imagine, the leader who rarely raises any concerns when you meet in person. Then, when you are more than at an arm's length distance, s/he finds the satisfaction of composing, and addressing you with insulting emails — a proper lesson in how to perform as a leader if you want to demoralize and demotivate a subordinate.

To be able to function as a productive leader, rule number one is to surround yourself with top people. This is hardly a unique statement, however there is nothing more gratifying than knowing that all your department heads in the hotel are first-class. This should be very high on any GM's agenda. Not only are you safeguarding a smooth operation, but as importantly, you make life as a GM much more efficient and enjoyable.

Top people need top salaries and benefits, hence, compensate them well. I know one successful GM who took this approach to the extreme. "I pay the highest salaries in town, and I have, in relation to the size and facilities of the hotel, the highest number of employees." With this approach, his hotel was the most attractive hotel employer in town, and he could hand-pick the best applicants, resulting in outstanding service delivery. However, there are dangerous salary implications if the competitors apply the same recruiting strategy.

When I moved back to Phuket in 2014 as Area GM of South Thailand for the Anantara brand of Minor Hotels, I was also GM of the beautiful Anantara Phuket Villas. This is an 87-key pool villa resort on Mai Khao beach, located on the island's west coast. I would describe it as 5-star+. Despite the limited size of the resort, and despite the fact that I had a first-class Executive Assistant Manager in Christian Gerart, I was not 100% satisfied with the standard of the overall service. As Area GM you also have extra pressure. It's not sustainable to push GMs reporting to you if your own KPI performances are not amongst the best. I said to myself, and Christian, that I wanted the best staff on the Island, that's it. I did not start with specific positions, I started with an individual that I knew would make a difference.

Khun Yah, the most professional guest contact person that I have ever seen in action. When I left Sheraton Phuket, 3 ½ years earlier, she oversaw the 52 "Pool Villas" within the resort. She had moved to another Starwood resort in Phuket, now being Front Office Manager at the Westin. We paid her what she was asking for to join us and created (!) a service executive position. With her focus on guest satisfaction, she masterminded change in Anantara Phuket Villas. Her way of engaging her team members and making sure that they together looked after the wellbeing of every single guest was simply outstanding. Khun Yah's genuine and profound way of caring for our guests was contagious and could soon be felt in the entire resort. It took nine months, and the resort was, for the first time in its seven-year history, number one in RevPar in the comp set. A lot thanks to the fantastic reviews we received on all social media platforms. This would not have been the case without Khun Yah. A good example that it pays off to pay for the best.

Knowing when and how to delegate is an art in itself. To delegate is to allocate responsibility. I can admit that sometimes it's also to clean the desk of boring working tasks that can be performed by someone else. As GM, I was always fortunate, or made sure, to have a very good "no.2", i.e., Hotel Manager, Resident Manager or Executive Assistant Manager. Their aim is to become GM, and therefore it's to their benefit to perform certain working tasks that normally would be the responsibility of the GM.

The best training is to put someone outside their comfort zone, that's what delegation often is all about. When setting deadlines for a working task, make sure that you provide a comfortable margin. Nothing is more embarrassing than having to ask your boss for more time. Support and show interest in the task that has been delegated, and occasionally follow up, without micromanaging. This is important, though sometimes there's a thin line.

The team spirit is as important, if not more, than the individual associates with great skills and experience. How to establish a good team spirit? Each department head is responsible for its team, however the GM can contribute in many ways. Be visible in the daily operation and show interest in what's going on, and how individual associates are doing and feeling. Show your face and show concern. It is important not to forget the back of the house. Then it's the closest co-workers to the GM, department heads and members of the executive committee. The best team spirit I have experienced was at the Sheraton Grande Laguna Phuket. We became a team of hard-working friends. Importantly, not one day passed without a few good laughs. How much easier life is when you are having fun!

The executive committee had two distinctively different, but important regular meetings. One was a formal quarterly meeting where we reviewed all aspects of the hotel operation and related issues. Nothing hidden, everything on the table – transparency. These meetings usually took place in a competing resort. The reason for this was twofold. Firstly, by leaving the day-to-day working environment, the whole set-up indicates a sense of extra importance, a full day away. Secondly, we could always learn something from the competition regarding meeting facilities, F&B quality, and service. Then we had a far more non-formal, very casual, meeting. The members of the executive committee could on a random Friday receive an SMS saying, for example: "Crisis Meeting, parking at 16.00." The sender was me. No one would miss out on a "Crisis Meeting," and they would all be punctual. As a GM, it's nice to find an interest besides work that could be enjoyed by everyone and improve the team spirit. At the parking lot we decided which beach bar should be the meeting point. If the mutual interest is chilled Cloudy Bay, so be it. We had some great gatherings, usually starting with a bit of business talk, fast-changing to anything but business talk. A bunch of colleagues enjoying each other's company, team spirit at its best. Important, as the GM you are always the leader, and when needed, there is no doubt who calls the shots.

As a leader it's important to allocate ample time for direct reports. Do it when you really can focus on the person seeking your attention and support. How often haven't you heard comments like: "Anything important, I have a meeting in 5 minutes?" or "Make it quick please, I need to make an urgent call," or....you get the point. When I called one specific boss, and he was short of time, he could say: "Jan, I'll call you back in one hour, if OK with you, I am then free to talk." He would call me at the agreed time, and even though he had around 20 direct reports, it felt like I was the one and only. He took time when he had time to focus 100% on me and my concerns. It sounds basic, it is basic, but it is not always the case. "Open door policy" – yes, if you close the laptop and can give full attention to the person visiting.

In my introduction I am referring to Marc McCormack and his book "What they don't teach you at Harvard Business School". In this book, McCormack refers to three "hard-to-say phrases." *I don't know.* As a GM it's impossible to know everything about everything. It's natural not to have all the answers in such a diverse business. If you don't know, give guidance on how to find an answer or a solution. *I need help.* "Same, same," and your co-workers love to assist the boss. It can also be helpful to make a telephone call to a fellow GM. Many times, this can be extremely valuable. *I was wrong.* Don't bury a mistake or a wrong judgment. In addition, it can lead to hesitation in trying something new, not to have a failure. "Avoiding past mistakes" is one way of defining experience. There will be no mistakes if you do not have the guts to try something new. Don't be afraid of these phrases, they can often be your savior. They also refer strongly to the important behavior of being transparent.

The more you communicate, the more information you will receive. As GM, it isn't enough to be present in daily morning meetings. Make sure to make it a point to sit in at departmental meetings, rotate. Learn what happens in a specific department and communicate about what's happening in the rest of the organization. I think this is far better than the frequently used "Town Hall" meetings, where all associates are gathered, however, one way doesn't exclude the other. At the Sheraton Amman we implemented "GM's Corner". This was a big poster outside the staff canteen where I communicated various issues of importance to all associates. The content was changed minimum on a monthly basis, and when I was not creative enough, I "rented out" the space to Francois Waller, Resident Manager. This was a way to keep everyone up to date on all (nearly) important matters concerning the hotel.

Be visible towards all stakeholders. As a GM, it's a must to be visible. I know a Managing Director who once told me: "I have good Managers in place in all three hotels, so I can run the business from home by analyzing the figures and KPIs." In any business, how can you analyze figures if you do not know in detail the product generating the figures? It's non-debatable, the GM must be visible towards associates, guests, suppliers, and owners. As earlier stated, a hotelier should ideally be a bit of an exhibitionist.

Building relationships is a "chain reaction". The base for building relationships is to always be transparent. Transparency is to be honest, open, frank, and clear in communication. If you, as a leader, consistently interact in a transparent way, you will receive the same from your co-workers and trust will be established. Trust with time will generate loyalty, the ultimate relationship. Transparency generates trust that generates loyalty. What more can you ask for as a leader, as a GM?

Leadership also entails to supervise and masterminding *change.* In the office of a GM colleague I could read the following on a framed piece of art: "*Rewrite the Rules, Always*". She elaborated about her cardinal rule and said: "Too many times we continue doing what we have done in the past without really thinking if it adds value. Is this process still valid and how can we do it better, both in regard to the guest experience and/or the most efficient way to do it? In most cases, it's just common sense" (which is not very common – my comment).

"I love change," sorry to say, but this is one of the most common lies in business. The vast majority prefers to conduct business exactly the same way today as they did yesterday. Change is therefore often a huge challenge. To succeed, the GM has to embrace, and be the force behind, any change in the hotel.

Opening

Are the same management and leadership qualities applicable when you oversee an opening as GM?

There are literally hundreds of tasks to keep track of during the pre-opening and opening phases of a hotel. One could therefore easily draw the conclusion that managerial skills, e.g., as mentioned initially in this chapter, planning, organizing, and coordinating resources to manage tasks and deliver results, would be the most important. Action plans covering every detail of an opening are easily available to support the planning. No need to re-invent the wheel. There is no doubt that managerial skills are crucial though I would say that leadership skills are just as essential.

I have personally been involved in the opening of three Sheraton hotels: Oslo (Norway) as Director of Sales, Antalya (Turkey) as Resident Manager and the Algarve (Portugal) as Resident Manager. It's during the pre-opening phase that the GM "builds the team" and the team spirit. Kai Mikkelsen, GM in Oslo, was a master in following up on all managerial details while simultaneously having the leadership skills to make a hard-working team bond. He knew how to build relationships and create a team spirit that carried over to the post-opening days.

Most hotel openings are "soft," i.e., often with a limited number of rooms ready to be occupied and not all restaurants and other facilities fully operational. The Sheraton Hotel Oslo Fjord was always set to open on March 01, 1985. It opened as planned on that Friday with all rooms and all other facilities fully operational. To top it off, we had 250 invited guests the same afternoon for the official inauguration, followed by a gala dinner for 100 VIPs. If anything, a "hard opening." Hat off to the contractor, the owner, and the GM. The GM's management skills AND leadership made sure that operationally we were set to go exactly as planned. If you, as a hotel school student, can arrange for a hotel opening as a traineeship, you have scored gold. You will benefit from a unique experience.

The Mirror

Mirror, mirror on the wall.... What do you see, and more importantly, what do the associates see when looking at their GM? An energetic and passionate person who loves the job should ideally be the answer. Personally, I was sometimes too casual in my behavior and I therefore, in certain camps, was considered to be too laid back. Never forget, perception is reality.

Occasionally it's OK to have an extra drink with your boss or peers, but not often, rather go to bed. You do not want to be known as the "Party animal." Last, but not least, as GM, you are a role model for all associates, and this is also applicable outside the hotel premises.

As a side comment, an interesting observation is the way many GMs communicate when you haven't seen her/him for some time. It's business straight away, nothing about the family or the vacation, no let's talk RevPar, GOP%, compset ranking or any other KPI. This comes in combination with the "**I and WE Syndrome**" - If the hotel is doing fine, it's "**I**" am doing great business, if the hotel is not doing too good, it's "**WE**" have a bit of a problem. Hoteliers are daily fed with results and comparisons with the previous year, budget, forecast, compset, maybe that's the reason for the, to me, sometimes strange behavior.

The Question

Many times, I have heard colleagues say: "He or she is a very good operator" or "She or he is a very good GM." What does it take to be a first-class GM? Which criteria must be fulfilled to be considered a good GM? Does it differ if you own the hotel and you are the GM, or you are engaged by an owner to be GM, or you are representing a management company to be the GM, or you are the GM of a franchised hotel, or.......?

Depending on the "structural position" of the GM, some issues will be tackled differently, however, to be a good operator/hotelier / GM, certain "attributes" are a must – A professional hotelier is a professional hotelier!

Give me 3 criteria for being successful as a GM. This is what I asked several GMs and corporate executives, current and retired, to provide me with. This was not an attempt to conduct a sophisticated survey, by any means, only to collect the thoughts from a few hoteliers, some more experienced than others, with combined working fields in Europe,

Africa, the Middle East, Asia, and the USA. As an interesting comparison, I also received input from hotel school students. You will find all 15 answers in appendix 2.

In an effort to shortly summarize, **being former hoteliers, current hoteliers or future hoteliers, the ability to deal with people, being associates, owners or guests, is a red thread.**

Empathy, passion, empowerment, motivation, training/development, results, lead by example, communication, and integrity are just some key words. Noteworthy that no one has mentioned anything about "technical skills" or suggested background, e.g., F&B, sales, finance. **This is a "people's business" and the recipe for being successful as a GM seems to be strong personal leadership skills that will lead to happy associates, happy guests, happy bottom line, and happy owners**. These are just a few comments to the answers, which should be worthwhile reading for a future GM (and current). There is a wealth of experience to draw from. Once again, this is input from a random population of hoteliers, though combined I would think it represents a vast majority.

What I have learned

Open the wallet and make sure to surround yourself with top people.

Be yourself with the understanding that different people need to be treated differently and your behavior must be flexible to adapt to different cultures. This refers to emotional intelligence.

"Be yourself; everyone else is already taken."— Oscar Wilde

Build relationships. Transparency generates trust that generates loyalty.

Show respect. When colleagues need your advice and support, make sure to allocate ample time.

Delegate. It's not primarily to off-load yourself as GM, it's good training for your subordinates to occasionally be outside their comfort zone.

Be visible and communicate. It's the best way of obtaining feedback from guests and associates.

Technology - or pure operational changes can often face resistance. To succeed, the GM has to embrace, and be the force behind, any change in the hotel.

Be caring. Also be empathetic to issues that can

occur outside working hours. Quoting my Marriott friend in Jordan, Philip Papadopoulos: "Connecting with associates through the power of care."

Guts. Don't be afraid of asking for help or admitting mistakes or lack of knowledge.

Decision making. Discuss issues, ask for advice, however, as the leader be firm, and ideally fast, in making decisions. Indecision creates frustrations, loss of respect and credibility amongst co-workers.

The "I and We Syndrome" - Avoid it.

Never lose track of the bottom line. You are paid to make a satisfactory return to the investors/owners. Take this into consideration for every cent that you spend (over the years, I have buried many purchasing requests in my top right drawer) and stay on top of the revenue stream, i.e., keep a close eye on sales, distribution, and marketing activities.

Look after the hotel assets. You are the custodian of a multi-million-dollar property. Ask yourself: "If I leave tomorrow, will the hotel be in as good, or better, condition as the day I arrived as GM?" Be your own asset manager.

Passion. This cannot be taught. However, you

are hardly a hotelier if you are not passionate about the hotel business. Show it, show energy. When passionate about your work, it will be reflected in the way you treat your associates and the way they treat you, most importantly, the way the associates treat the guests. It means a lot!

"**A customer-driven company** is one that recognizes that its only true asset is satisfied customers." However, you can only generate satisfied guests if you have **satisfied associates, *the by far most important asset.***

A sense of humor is important. A good laugh makes daily life so much more enjoyable.

SALES AND MARKETING

As indicated, the GM must be "in the mix" when it relates to sales and marketing (S&M). I started my hotel life in sales, though today's sales activities, especially distribution, have changed dramatically since my days. Being perceived as a "sales and marketing guy," still I cannot give a lot of advice as this part of the business continues to develop with such tremendous speed.

Technology has changed the way we see daily business, check-in/out processes, lock devices, payment methods, purchasing procedures, restaurant reservations and so on. However, the most significant evolution in the hotel industry over the last four decades is the way we attract guests to our hotels. We have always offered the best product and service possible, however it is a profound change in the way we conduct S&M. It has become more diverse, more technical, more specialized, and fewer room nights are being generated based on personal contacts and relationships. The landscape has totally changed, and little remains of the most traditional sales activity, to meet clients face-to-face and negotiate deals. What used to be my forte is now of more marginal interest. Rightly or wrongly so.

Why even have a chapter related to S&M if I have little to contribute? *The reason*: To highlight that you will not become a successful GM if you do not have control over S&M! It can also, hopefully, be of interest to have a bit of comparison with "the old days." Let's be clear, having a firm grip over S&M does not mean that you will become more than an average GM, it's a basic requirement.

Maybe because of my background in sales, I have always had a focus on S&M. As of my first GM position in Hammamet, I implemented a daily sales meeting to follow the morning meeting. As much as the GM needs to make certain of a daily smooth operation, as important is it to daily review and support the S&M activities. It's a "360" – A world-class operation is a waste if potential guests and clients are not aware of your hotel and services, world class S&M is a waste if the operation is not up to standard.

Ecommerce (including OTAs), social media, revenue management, influencers, seamless upselling, RFPs, sophisticated loyalty programs, CRM, AI..... These have all appeared and been developed, in different time frames, since the 1990s. As we look back a bit and get the development in perspective, one wonders how the S&M tool kit will look in the mid and long-term future!

When I joined Sheraton Stockholm as Sales Executive in 1982, we printed a rate sheet twice a year, this must be the true definition of revenue management! We had weekend packages as a complement and Sheraton was the first hotel in Stockholm, soon to be copied, and probably the first city hotel in Europe, that combined accommodation with destination attractions, museums, amusement parks, sightseeing plus transportation. This was the embryo of what later became "Destination Stockholm," comprising a variety of hotels and attractions which was replicated in many major cities. What might be hard to believe for today's sales executives is the way we promoted our packages. What to do when you do not have Internet and OTAs that can be your distribution channels? Our most important markets where the cities up north in Sweden, where the retail travel agents (the ones that used to be strategically located on street corners!) combined a return bus trip, meals and the Sheraton weekend package.

Flight from Stockholm up north with excess luggage of brochures, rental car and off I went, sometimes in snow and minus 20 degrees Celsius. City after city, retailer after retailer, distributing Sheraton weekend brochures and making sure that they had the best display in the stores. These retail agents became my friends, and I timed the visit to the most important one, Erik Brännström of Resespecialisterna in Piteå (850 km north of Stockholm), to have lunch, go fishing together, dinner with him and his wife in their house, overnight, then in the car early the following morning. When I later saw that the occupancy a few weekends ahead looked soft, I knew what to do. A telephone call to Erik in Piteå, or any of his colleagues up north, informing about the dates and confirming a few hundred dollars in advertising support. This was the recipe to get two busloads of guests for the desired weekend. A story of the sales life prior to the Internet. However, I think that a worthwhile takeaway is that a lot of business can still be generated based on personal relationships, even though the retailer on the street corner is gone.

Another story from "the old days". During my time in Gothenburg, Sweden, I took part in creating, what I at least initially thought, a very smart and creative package. Gothenburg was the epicenter of Volvo cars, with HQ and a mega factory. The package was aimed at the US market. You fly to Gothenburg with SAS Airline, buy your Volvo car, drive around in Scandinavia staying at the Sheraton hotels (in those days Stockholm, Oslo, Malmo, Gothenburg, and Copenhagen), also with overnight at the famous Swedish glass factories. Your trip ends in Gothenburg, from where the car will be shipped to the USA. Why would a Volvo car buyer from the USA bother? At least in those days, if you bought the car in Sweden and before shipping it home, you drove a certain number of miles, being covered in our suggested route, you did not have to pay sales tax. The whole excursion to Scandinavia, including flights and accommodation would be paid for. We collaborated with a Scandinavian tour operator specialized in the US market. I do not remember how they marketed and distributed our beautiful brochures, but the success rate of room nights and cars sold was easily counted—zero!

Whatever product, whatever level of demand, distribution is the key to success. If we had had the Internet and social media to lean on, I am sure that Volvo would have been forced to speed up their assembly line at the plant in Gothenburg.

In the local market, with sales calls, the GM can generate a lot of business; conferences, banquets, and outside catering, in addition to room nights from corporate accounts. Whenever, wherever there are face-to-face interactions with clients, the GM can be the "closing factor." During my first four weeks as GM of the Sheraton in Amman, I did two joint sales calls with our Director of Sales daily to corporate accounts, embassies, and "influencers". It soon bore fruit and it helped me to feel comfortable in a new business environment and in my new hometown. I have earlier mentioned that a telephone call can be a secret weapon relating to complaints. It will be no surprise, it is also a great tool to generate sales. If the sales department has a lead for an important piece of business and the potential client receives a telephone call, or request for a Zoom meeting, from the GM assuring her/his personal commitment (!) to make the event a success, you will most probably close the deal.

Nowadays we take for granted receiving daily

comparisons of occupancy and average rate of our main competitors. RevPar, the worldwide accepted KPI for comparison, is a measure that came about at the beginning of the millennium. As a result, this is when a number of independent 3rd party companies, gathering, comparing and communicating the figures, were established. A bit more efficient than the associates of the hotels' switchboards calling each other in the early morning checking occupancies. I also remember a measure from long before the RevPar, i.e., Single Potential Rate. The total room revenue was calculated based on full house with single occupancy (easy to calculate with the famous rate sheet as cheat sheet). The actual total room revenue was then calculated as a percentage of "the maximum room revenue with single occupancy."

The importance of revenue management cannot be underestimated. The bi-annual printing of rate sheets has been substituted by sometimes bi-hourly rate changes. Enough said, it's a "no-brainer" that the GM needs to be heavily involved in the rate strategy. The airline industry started with this art of pricing. Normally they have fewer competitors to worry about, though more variables to keep track on, with connecting flights to take into consideration. They are still ahead of the hotel industry in terms of sophisticated software and revenue management strategies.

"Don't put all eggs in one basket", this is as valid today as ever. A classic is the 80/20 rule (also called the Pareto Principle), meaning that 80 percent of your sales is generated by 20 percent of your clients. This ratio might be acceptable, but you definitely need to change sales strategy if you're in the area of 90/10, ideally before.

The popular subject of OTAs. I fully agree that life as a GM, or Chief Marketing Officer, would be far better if all the business from OTAs instead were generated through your own website. Today, it's not the case, and it will never be the case. OTAs are here to stay. Back in time, we used to give the major tour operators 20-25 percent off rack rates/listed rates, which might still be the case. In addition, often a financial contribution to secure a half-page, or full page, in their program. A limited number of brochures were printed and distributed to a limited number of retailers in a limited geographical area. Then we sat back hoping for room nights to materialize. Not to forget occasional fam trips by retail agents. Today, a hotel belonging to one of the major international chains pays the OTAs around 15% in commission, whilst an independent hotel will pay around the 20% mark, sometimes more. Maybe the comparison with tour operators is not fully adequate, however, most importantly the OTAs offer worldwide distribution. Once again, OTAs are here to stay, hence as you cannot beat them, I suggest joining them. Aim to be featured on the first 2-3 pages even if it costs you another couple of % in commission. For an independent, non-chain affiliated hotel, there isn't much of an option if you want to challenge the big chains. Empty hotel rooms collecting dust has never been a profitable strategy. Unfortunately, not even consistently great reviews are a guarantee for a prominent placement. One saving grace seems to be a trend by potential guests to first check hotels and rates on OTA platforms and thereafter make the actual booking on the hotel website.

As per H2c's 2023 Digital Hotel Operations Study, bookings through OTAs were down from 39% in 2022 to 34% in 2023, while direct bookings increased from 20% to 29% over the same period (based on feedback from 84 hotel chains representing 17,406 properties with more than 2 million rooms). The same report credits the result in part to "quality content on brand websites, loyalty offers and an increasing customer focus using smart and agile systems." (PhocusWire) Make sure that you have an up-to-date and very user-friendly website and a well-functioning CRM system.

97% of millennials use social media to share pictures of their trips. (Influencer Marketing Hub) Some amazing figures of TikTok, according to a study by MGH, a US marketing communications agency specializing in tourism marketing. Along with inspiring people to visit new destinations, TikTok, with 150 million users in the USA, also motivates people to visit specific hotels/resorts or attractions they've seen on the app. Approximately 32% said they had booked a stay at a new hotel/resort they saw on TikTok. (Hotels Mag, 2023) 2022 statistics give at hand that there are 4.8 billion (!) social media users worldwide, representing 59.9% of the global population and 92.7% of all internet users. (Search Engine Journal) This highlights the enormous power of social media. A well-executed marketing strategy on social media should be a priority of any hotel or resort.

Awards, awards and awards – "We are thrilled to announce that our hotel has been awarded..." How many different hotel awards are there and how reliable are these "surveys"? If you operate a top-class hotel or resort, you do not have to beg readers on social media to vote for you. You will fill your rooms and restaurants with satisfied guests, being the best promoters there are.

Now a story which justifies my skepticism towards the multitude of awards. In the airline industry, since a long time, the awards perceived as the most prestigious and most reliable are probably the ones awarded by Skytrax. We have all seen how airlines promote the fact that they have been voted the best airline in the world, the best regional airline, having the best airline crew and so on. A big Skytrax logo is usually featured in a prominent area of the promotional pieces of the airlines, often on mega billboards by the airports. These awards also cover airports and airport lounges, and not to forget airport hotels. 2011 was the first year of the airport hotel category, which coincided with my arrival as GM of Regal Airport Hotel in Hong Kong. As soon as I found out about this new category, I put the sales machinery in top gear. All available contacts of the hotel's sales department, and all contacts of the corporate sales office, were emailed with a nice message asking for their support. We succeeded – "the best airport hotel in the world", in the world! We ran quite a smooth operation, however, as GM I can honestly say that if this, close to 1,100 room airport hotel would be the best in its category worldwide, the hotel industry faced a problem. To be honored with a nice award, regardless of service level experienced by passengers/guests, maybe (?) the key factor is who can initiate the best "recruiting campaign". I left Hong Kong in 2012, proud to have been GM of "the best airport hotel in the world" for two consecutive years.

What I have learned

Sales and marketing, a must for the GM to be up to date and be actively involved.

"**Sales interaction**" to be a natural ingredient in the GM's daily work, i.e., to interact with in-house conference organizers and key persons of the companies / organizations hosting conferences. Also to attend feedback meetings with conference organizers.

Sales calls by the GM in the local market, and at trade shows, will generate a lot of room nights.

To close a deal, the GM can often be the recipe to success.

GM's daily sales meeting is probably the most important meeting of the day. 15-20 minutes of full focus to generate business.

OTAs are here to stay, hence take advantage of them.

The website to be constantly updated and to be extremely user-friendly.

The impact and power of social media is tremendous – To be an obvious reflection in the marketing plan.

Risk spreading. Make sure to diversify the client base. Analyze each market segment and the geographical spread/point of sales of your accounts.

Listen before talking, the virtue of any efficient salesperson.

Awards left, right and centre, to be taken with a pinch of salt.

Sales and Marketing, a must for the GM to be up to date and be actively involved!

HUMAN RESOURCES

Let me first express my admiration for everyone who has joined the hotel industry in the human resources field. I say this because, not only in sales, but also within the HR department, there is an "80/20 ratio." At least that's how I assess the workload. If you disregard the part relating to training, most often under the hat of HR, 80 would represent the 80% of the daily workload that revolves around problems, and the remaining 20% would represent positive interactions and encounters. This equates to a tough working environment and only the strongest survive as a true HR professional. It's not for the faint-hearted.

Director of HR

What characterizes the true HR professional in a hotel? To me, the ideal individual should be someone who has, amongst others, a background in hotel operations to better understand the challenges and possibilities at hand; an experienced person able to deal with all levels of the organization, calm and collected, and a good listener. Integrity and confidentiality are incredibly important for the person in this role.

I appreciate seeing the HR responsible around and about in the hotel, communicating and obtaining a true feeling for the working conditions of all associates. Together with the GM, the person who can take the pulse of the overall "state of affairs." A challenge for the Director of HR (DOHR) is to avoid getting stuck in administration, daily routines and "fire brigade management." Recruitment, union relations, a safe working environment, and employee benefits are some of the important responsibilities of the DOHR, however, to look ahead and develop associates through appropriate and professional training must always be on top of the agenda.

Training

In any hotel you will find departmental training sessions. My experience tells me that there isn't enough "specially designed" training, i.e., specific training programs for individuals with the aim to prepare them for their next step or steps in the industry. Looking back on the training that took place in my hotels as GM, we did not conduct the training the way I would implement it today. Basic departmental training is an important necessity, being "classroom style" or on-the-job training. Depending on the size of the hotel, I would then have one to three associates from each department on "tailor made training", i.e., a detailed program to prepare them for the next stage(s) in their career, which has been outlined by themselves with support of the DOHR. There should be a formalized development plan, supported by individual training, for the associates who are determined to make the hotel life their future. Time is a scarce resource, and also sometimes commitment. There has to be 100% commitment from everyone involved, including concerned department heads, who occasionally have to manage the operation without certain associates being in training.

Critical is also the onboarding. The hotel must make you feel welcomed and "wanted" as of your first working day and a detailed and meaningful onboarding/training program should be in place. As an introduction to the hotel industry, I have a strong memory of tidying up the mess in the F&B

manager's office during my onboarding week at the Sheraton Stockholm Hotel. A truly different way of being introduced to the world of culinary art.

What surprised me when working for a big international chain like Sheraton/Starwood was the lack of focus and training of "No. 2s", being an important part of the future of the company. It was given very little attention from the corporate office.

Training and succession planning at a corporate level are obviously as important as they are on a hotel level. During my six and a half years as Executive Assistant Manager/Resident Manager with Sheraton, I only experienced one course specially designed for the preparation to become GM. As second in command, you were very much relying on the goodwill of the GM to prepare you for the next important step. Your future was also 100% dependent on the evaluation by your GM. Without her/his blessing, you would not move forward. This will probably never change – your GM "can make or break" your future, do not forget.

Starwood later implemented a "Mentor / Mentee program" with a designated GM as the mentor to a Resident Manager, the mentee, in a sister hotel. I had the privilege of twice being a mentor, though I was not too much in favor of the set-up as I sometimes felt that I was intervening in the responsibilities of the GM of the mentee. At least the program demonstrated attention to the future of the company. Not that I can take any credit whatsoever, but it's nice to see that both my mentees have done very well with their hotel careers. One as a corporate executive in the hotel and gaming industry, one with Marriott as a successful GM.

Appraisals

Appraisals – important or a necessary evil? For many, the latter, but the answer is: extremely important! Here are a few tips:

- In addition to a formal yearly appraisal, make sure to once a quarter, or once a trimester, give as detailed feedback as possible to your direct reports. Maybe more informal sessions. It might sound too frequent, but it is worth the time and effort for both parties. From what I understand, many companies have abandoned formal appraisal cycles, instead focusing on instant feedback. I personally believe in formal appraisals, however this should obviously not replace important instant feedback.

- Take the opportunity to also discuss career

plans, as well as plans for the department in question.

- Get away from the hotel environment to a quiet and neutral place.

- Make sure that you have allocated enough time. For many, appraisal sessions are the most important meetings of the year. You should give them your full focus.

- Self-evaluation as a basis for the discussion can be very helpful and productive.

- It's also the time to find out what's required of you as a boss to support in the daily challenges, and necessary support for the colleague's development.

- If you want specific areas to be improved, you cannot be too general. Make sure to exemplify mistakes made or actions not to have been taken and highlight the results not being achieved (and achieved!). An action plan for development should be mutually agreed upon.

- It's not only what your impressions are as the boss, what about feedback from the colleagues and subordinates of the person being appraised? Your own observations and input from DOHR should be sufficient to initiate a meaningful discussion. Many chain hotels perform yearly a "360 survey" which provides a lot of valuable information about all department heads and their leadership.

- An appraisal session should be motivational, that's the overall objective!

I enjoyed discussing the daily operation and challenges with all my subordinates even though the formal appraisal was never my favorite engagement. Most challenging was the process as AGM, as you didn't see the GMs in action during the daily operation. Unfortunately, the status of KPIs played too important a role. However, I had seven GMs to evaluate, and saw them face-to-face quite regularly, hardly what you can do as an AGM if you have 20-25 GMs spread around geographically.

Recruiting

Considering myself being a person with limited patience, I was good at taking my time in the recruiting process. It's too costly and too risky if you are not confident in hiring a person of the right caliber. This could even result in a key position being vacant for quite some time. If so, it signals to all involved the importance of the position. There is always the parachute in a probation period, however considerable damage will be caused if you must start the hiring process all over again.

The CV - History of positions, employer and timing is obviously of major importance and is usually the criteria in the first screening process. Then, the interesting references. Will you find a referee that would not recommend the candidate in question? Maybe one in hundred. Why would anyone name a referee on their CV who would not give the potential employer positive feedback? It took me a few years too many before I came to the insight that it is extremely valuable to seek information from people who have had the candidate as their boss. The true picture will then come to light. It is rare to see subordinates as referees on a CV, hence you must use your network in a discrete way. The hotel industry might not exactly be a duck pond, but not much larger, so with patience (!), you will be able to find the info you are looking for.

Sometimes you can read, or rather interpret, from a CV that a candidate did not leave an employer out of their own will. It is rare to leave a job without having a new one lined up. Sometimes there are gaps in a CV being "covered" in a strange way. Let's make a clear statement: there isn't something necessarily wrong with being forced to leave an employer. There can be a multitude of reasons and many of them should not reflect negatively on a candidate, sometimes to the contrary. It is far better to be honest and transparent than trying to hide facts.

It's impossible to cover the topic of recruiting without touching on the subject of quotas. In the Gulf states, there are quotas based on nationality as the governments are pushing for locals to enter the workforce of the private sector. It's Saudization, Omanization, Bahranization, to name a few. These quotas determine the percentage of the employer's workforce that must comprise local nationals. A hotter subject is quotas based on gender. There are strong arguments on both sides of the aisle. My take is simple: the available position to be filled with the best-suited candidate, gender should not play a role in the selection process.

A classic question: to hire based on skills or attitude? For associates with guest contact, attitude will win over skills, though ideally the answer is both attitude and skills. Attitude also entails the way you act towards your colleagues, not only towards guests. However, certain positions are impossible to hire only based on attitude. You can have a great team of smiling and courteous associates in the finance department. Without being "figure savvy," you will soon deeply regret the recruiting process. I do not know the criteria when the hiring of the female associates took place for the opening of Sheraton Gothenburg in Sweden. When I arrived, as Director of Sales, one year after the opening, my first thought was that the overriding criteria must have been "looks". Amazingly, they could all have been on the cover of any glossy fashion magazine.

My favorite part of the recruiting process was the face-to-face interviews. "Within the first 7 seconds of meeting, people will have a solid impression of who you are." (Rural Lifestyle Dealer) Tough for an eager candidate who wants to make a great first impression. I have been interviewed a fair number of times. The most common questions have been: "What are your strengths, what are your weaknesses?" I think anyone preparing for an interview will have answers to these two questions. When interviewing, I used to ask the same, but in a different way, which I think gives more "trustworthy" answers. Something like: "Let's assume that I, here and now offer you the job, and you accept. I would then tell you that during the first six months you should not come to work. Instead, you have a free budget to attend any training available worldwide to better prepare yourself for your upcoming position in this hotel. What three subjects would you prioritize?" A more subtle way to have eventual weaknesses recognized and a fun exercise.

Qualifications, references, appearance, skills, attitude – a big mix of facts and impressions need to be considered before reaching a final decision on which candidate to recruit. The expression "chemistry" has various definitions; to me, it's the feeling of a person having the same values, that you are on the same "wavelength." You feel a connection with the candidate "I can relate to and work with this person." It's hard to describe, but to me, this "chemistry" is of utmost importance and can sometimes compensate for some eventual shortcomings.

Time for headhunters, or recruiters. This is yet another 80/20, i.e., 80% hate, 20% love. The 20% relates to the one time a recruiter assisted me in finding the right candidate as my Executive Assistant Manager at the Sheraton Soma Bay in Egypt. Surprisingly, Sheraton was not able to provide candidates with the right talent. I am repeatedly talking about transparency and trust; these words are not always applicable to headhunters. I do not know how many times I was contacted by "friends" in the recruiting business asking for assistance in finding candidates for certain positions. Almost every time I was able to recommend professional candidates that I knew. On a few occasions, the same person, who even financially benefited from my support, tried to recruit executives from my hotel. Hardly what is expected from a "loyal" business partner, and the reason for the 80%. Check with friends in the business for suitable leads and make sure to explore all options before burdening your P&L with a headhunter. Many (most?) of them are posting career opportunities on social media. Your HR department can do the same.

Work Ethics

As a GM you must have 100% discipline in conducting the daily business. Discipline in the sense of honesty, integrity, being responsible and accountable.

The responsibility is exposed in various ways. As highlighted, the GM is the role model, and stepping outside the boundaries of the norm of proper work ethics will have huge negative repercussions, with instant “ripples in the water”. Being late to work, or meetings, sounds “innocent”, however if that’s the way the GM acts, which indicates lack of respect and responsibility, soon no one will be on time!

Have I always stayed 100% within the framework of proper work ethics? Luckily no “80/20” this time, however in the beginning as GM, I might have been too generous in offering “friends and family rates” when welcoming friends. If full house, which probably was the case on some occasions, this equates to giving away the owner’s money and could have caused some awkward questions. What has to be considered as outside the boundaries of proper work ethics is how we once dealt with the water shortage whilst I was Resident Manager at the Sheraton Istanbul. The whole city was suffering and to safeguard enough water supply we, as all other hotels, had to rely on buying mountain water that was being delivered by a limited number of water trucks. When the Assistant Chief Engineer came to my office and proudly told me that he had kidnapped a water truck on its way to the Hilton hotel, I admit that I praised him and was proud of his initiative.

Always be aware that there is a lot of jealousy in the hotel. The GM has a nice car, brings home food and beverages, sometimes has accommodation in the hotel (nothing to be jealous about!), and gets to wine and dine in the restaurants. As a GM you have a lot of perks not to be misused. In Phuket I used to frequent the gym daily in the early afternoon, a bit of a dead time in the operation. Through the grapevine, I found out that the union representatives questioned that I was using the gym during "working hours". We evidently had a different perspective on the term "working hours". I didn't want the union to have anything "up their sleeve" on me, hence I went outside the hotel for my daily exercise. Also in Phuket, I now and then, in the early evening, gathered a couple of members of the executive committee for a beer or two in the bar, union again. However, one thing is to entertain guests or customers in the bar, another to have a drink with colleagues. Even though within the "ethic boundaries," it's a grey area as it doesn't look very professional and should be avoided.

A hotel has a mega number of contacts with different categories of suppliers. Never, ever, take advantage of your position in the hotel to obtain financial benefits from a supplier. There are many ways to induce the kiss of death. I know a GM that even used contacts with hotel suppliers to set up his own "side business". I was extra cautious when I was due to buy furniture for our newly bought house in Phuket. I knew very well that I could not price-wise take advantage of partners of the hotel, but maybe our purchasing manager could assist in contacting suppliers and make sure of speedy deliveries. I nearly felt paranoid about contacting the area HR responsible in writing with the question of whether it was OK to have her, the purchasing manager, help me. The issue was so sensitive that it traveled to the corporate office of Starwood in the USA. No worries, it was fine to have the purchasing manager helping, if it was outside normal working hours. In that respect, I must admit that a bit of cheating took place. She once came to my office with a quotation for a BBQ. The proforma indicated the price and then below in bold letters it said 50% discount and a new price. “Is the price fine with you?” she asked me. How easy it would have been to save some dollars, however with the risk of losing the job!

Another sensitive issue is to accept gifts. I am not talking about Christmas hampers or a bottle of wine, no, things of higher value. At the Sheraton Hammamet, we were the venue for a big conference organized by a major German tour operator, a daughter company of Lufthansa. We did our part to the great satisfaction of the client, and I received a fantastic present. Return business class tickets for me and Helle, Lufthansa network worldwide. I showed it to my boss, Sami Zoghbi, who said: "Great, well done." In response, I asked: "Would you mind signing the letter as your OK?" He happily did, and Helle and I could happily fly to South Africa, with little Victor in an extra complimentary business class seat. The signature was a blessing, my rear was covered.

Social media can also be related to work ethics. We all know that there is an issue with fake reviews. As an example, from the 30.2 million reviews posted on TripAdvisor in 2022, 4.4% were fake or fraudulent, according to the platform's Review Transparency Report released in April, 2023. There can be a temptation to initiate fake reviews on various platforms to improve ratings. For some this temptation has grown as many hotel chains over the years, as well as independent hotels, are linking parts of the yearly bonus scheme to ratings on specific social media platforms. I am a firm believer that there should not be anything related to financial incentives that in any way can be manipulated. 1.3 million fake reviews. How many were initiated by hoteliers? Work ethics!

I was once exposed to a very unusual situation. A middle-aged man approached me during dinner time outside our all-day restaurant at the Sheraton Soma Bay: "You're the GM, I'm checking out tomorrow, but I don't need an invoice." He was indirectly asking me to have his booking "disappear" and pay me directly, obviously anticipating a big discount. He was very calm and confident and I'm sure he had a good success rate in history. This was the only time that I had experienced such a request, and it was firmly rejected.

Work ethics also relates to the way you leave for another assignment. An executive chef, that I much appreciated, resigned to open his own restaurant. He asked me to cut his notice period short. I agreed, under the circumstance that he wouldn't "steal" any staff from the hotel to join his new adventure. I was naïve enough to trust a firm handshake. I don't remember the number of associates that left us, but it was both from the kitchen and service. Needless to say, I have never spent, and will never spend, a cent in his establishment.

"The way you leave is the way you will be remembered." This is correct, and this was highlighted to me by the chairman of Sheraton Amman Al Nabil Hotel & Towers, Mr. Nadim Mouasher.

Shortly after the tragic and devastating suicide bombings in three hotels in Amman, the Sheraton was the venue for an important charity dinner hosted by the Austrian Ambassador. To cancel or not to cancel was the question for quite some time. At the end, the event took place with security measures much tightened, e.g., the entrance of the hotel was corded off and no cars were allowed to park close by. We arranged for a provisional parking space on a big lawn a few hundred meters away from the hotel. At one stage, prior to dinner, I decided to have a walk to check that all was in good order at the car park. Outside the hotel I bumped into the CEO of Royal Jordanian Airlines with his wife, on their way to the charity dinner. He strongly expressed his discontent with the service of the parking. A lot of pressure had built up in preparation for this evening and I felt that if someone should be respectful of security precautions, even though not being offered 5-star service, it ought to be a top executive of an airline. It should be said that I, shortly prior to that evening, had used the service of Royal Jordanian on a visit to Thailand, my upcoming destination. The otherwise controlled GM "lost it!" "Maybe the parking service is as bad as the service I recently experienced on Royal Jordanian to Bangkok?" I retorted. Then a brisk walk to the parking lot to pick up my car and during the short drive home, I was fuming.

I was on my second Scotch when I had Mr. Mouasher on the phone. The gentleman in question had called him and complained about my behavior. Mr. Mouasher politely said something like: "Jan, you have such a good reputation, and you are soon going to leave Amman, don't destroy it, please apologize. The way you leave is the way you will be remembered." I swallowed the drink and Helle drove me back to the hotel. I waited until dinner was over. Now I swallowed my pride and apologized. It should be noted that there was nothing wrong with the service of Royal Jordanian. It was just a way for the defensive GM to dispose of his frustrations.

How is this story connected to work ethics? Your behavior as the boss, as GM, is 100 % related to work ethics, you must conduct yourself in a responsible way. If my move to Thailand hadn't been signed and sealed, maybe I would have reacted in a more polite manner (?), however, my uncontrolled behavior and comments, were a true low mark of my great time in a great city, in a great hotel. I am thankful for the call from Mr. Mouasher, and that I did swallow my pride and extended a well-deserved apology.

Regardless of circumstances, the lesson is to 100% "hang in there" until the last working day!

HR Reflections

Reflection – At least some HR related topics improve with time! Two short stories from the "old days", highlight the difference compared to today's more liberal thinking in most corners of the world.

In July 1992, one month prior to the opening of Sheraton Pine Cliffs in the Algarve, Helle arrived and moved in with me at my apartment in Pine Cliffs. As Resident Manager I had the privilege of being able to order food and beverage items from the hotel and pay the purchasing prices of the hotel. Very convenient and cheaper than the supermarket. Not to have any grey area, I addressed my new "family status" to the GM. I composed a formal memo (email did not exist!) with the subject "1 becomes 2" and inquired if my privilege of buying food from the hotel would also be applicable to my fiancée. The negative answer was a big disappointment; "At the end of the day you are not married" was the unexpected comment. "Fine, I'll divide my fridge so my fiancée doesn't drink any of my less expensive milk." I can, with certainty, assume that the GM's benefits included free food from the hotel, though I wonder how the goodies for the dog were accounted for. At a later stage my situation was "corrected", and we could drink from the same carton of milk.

A few years later, in 1994, Helle and I left the Algarve for my next assignment as Resident Manager of the Sheraton Istanbul Hotel. At this point in time, 2 had become 3, and a newborn Victor was a welcome addition to the family. Helle was still fiancée, no time for a wedding. In Istanbul we were living-in and as a benefit, we could have our meals in the hotel. However, this was a perk with a time limit. For Helle this benefit would cease after six months if we, at that point, would still not be married. The same also applied for her medical insurance. The benefits would only apply to Helle after six months if the situation was "being rectified"! We did rectify the situation. Luckily, our planned summer wedding fell within the stipulated deadline. Being married or not, these two memories highlight that society has changed quite a bit since the beginning of the 90s, at least in some parts of the world.

In the wake of the international hotel chains fast

growing their footprints, especially in mainland China, the demand for GMs has followed suit. Good news for today's hotel school students. Personally, I did 6 ½ years as Executive Assistant Manager / Resident Manager, nothing unique in the 80s and 90s, before I became GM. I was lucky to experience four hotels and five bosses during these years. What a great school in preparation for the GM assignment. I am not saying that the quality of first-time GMs is not of a high standard today, I am only pointing out that some might lack a bit of experience due to a common "fast-tracking" in the industry. I have mentioned that I did always benefit from having top-class number twos as well as pointing out that as number two, for the future, you are very much dependent on the support of your GM. It's therefore very gratifying for me to see all "my guys" as successful GMs.

The position of number two, being Executive Assistant Manager (EAM), Resident Manager (RM) or Hotel Manager (HM), is demanding and often underestimated. The title and responsibilities usually depend on the size of the hotel. Which, and how many, department heads report to you also determines the title. In big hotels there could, for example, be two EAMs in charge of different parts of the operation, e.g., EAM in charge of F&B and

EAM in charge of rooms. They would then report to the RM, in turn reporting to the GM. Hotels in general have anything but flat organization. This also means that the person on top of the hierarchy, the GM, is close to untouchable, the GM is the Queen or the King. For the second in command (going forward, let's assume the RM) the loyalty to the GM goes without saying.

With the big international hotel chains, the GM usually stands very strong. Strong as a boss in relation to the rest of the hotel team and, if there is a management agreement, strong as being appointed by the corporate office and approved by the owner. As RM, I experienced a situation when many, if not all, department heads had very negative opinions about the GM and I had to be the "cushion and calming factor", despite having the same feelings as my colleagues. My experience says that it's far better to ask for a transfer to another hotel than to take a fight with the GM.

I have sometimes reflected on the reason behind certain GMs being relocated to a specific hotel or resort. International hotel companies occasionally make, what at least look like, mistakes. To exemplify, how can a GM who doesn't like sunshine, sea, beach, kids, and golf be comfortable, and do a good job, as GM of a beach and golf resort? A GM of a Four Seasons, St. Regis, or Mandarin Oriental must know how to act, react, and be dressed to match the 5-star+ ambiance. This is most often the case, though I have seen some not-too-elegant mismatches.

Another reflection, probably far more interesting, is the criteria for appointing Area General Managers (AGM). I bet that 9 times out of 10, the most successful GMs in terms of financial results of their respective hotels will be the candidates for a vacant AGM position. Hopefully, I will lose this bet. Why? For the simple reason that area responsibilities take far more than successfully operating one hotel. From one day to the other, often what used to be your peers are now reporting to you. For many, a very difficult transition. Next challenge. From probably having established a good relationship with one owner, now dealing with, most often, a two-digit number of owners, another demanding challenge. I have no complaints regarding my AGMs over the years, on the contrary, however, I think that the described clearly illustrates that a successful GM, not necessarily will become a successful AGM.

Personally, I was new to Minor /Anantara hotels

when appointed AGM, i.e., no issue with former peers. In my first year, I exclusively worked with owned hotels in my area, and in the second year it was a mix of owned and managed hotels. I then had three owners to deal with. Having a total of seven hotels under my umbrella, one can easily say that this was a smooth transition from GM to AGM. Certain AGMs of international hotel chains are today responsible for 15 to 20 hotels and sometimes even more. One thing is for sure, as owner you will get far from the attention deserved and you must trust that the GM in charge of your hotel is of the highest standard. Referring to my earlier comment, a shrewd, maybe multiple hotel owner and a first-time GM might not be the preferred combination.

Some GMs obviously are of the right caliber to take on the AGM position. A very good example is Roeland Vos, who was a first-time GM at Sheraton Pine Cliffs in the Algarve, Portugal (having had the pleasure of me as RM), and during the period of eight years, climbed the ladder to become President for Starwood Europe. Shortly thereafter, he became President of Starwood Europe, Africa and the Middle East, a position he held for 12 years, before becoming CEO and thereafter, Chairman for Belmond. In addition to the qualities of a top-notch GM, Roeland obviously possesses unique leadership skills. He also knew how to balance the act of socializing with co-workers outside working hours, without losing the authority as the boss.

Reflecting on my hotel career, my proudest memory, which comes to mind during my random moments of being a bit "philosophical", dates back to my days at Sheraton Stockholm Hotel. After 18 months as a Sales Executive, I was promoted to Sales Manager. Shortly thereafter, the GM and AGM, Henry Hunold, advised me that he would put me on the schedule covering weekend duty management. This meant that, approximately once every two months, you lived-in from Friday night until Monday morning, overseeing the hotel, and representing the GM. I was not two years in the business and was made in charge of a 420-room hotel—at the time, the biggest in Sweden. The feeling of trust and responsibility given to me was overwhelming. This was the moment that convinced me that I had chosen the correct profession to pursue – my proudest moment as a hotelier.

What I have learned

The Director of HR to ideally have a

background in operations, being a person with “thick skin”.

A great responsibility lies on the GM and DOHR to support and facilitate the careers of young, aspiring hoteliers.

Training. In addition to departmental training, individual development plans are of utmost importance.

The first working day is maybe the most important. A professional and nice welcome to be prepared for the new co-worker, including a well-crafted onboarding program.

Appraisal is a process about past performance AND future plans. Take all the time needed. Think about how you want your boss to best perform your own appraisal and apply it to your direct reports. There can’t be any grey areas, be crystal clear in your feedback.

Recruiting

- **References**, obtain 360 feedback, i.e., not only from previous bosses, but also from subordinates.

- **You are better off leaving a position vacant** for a long period of time than hiring with uncertainty.

- **Attitude** always supersedes skills in the recruitment of guest contact associates.

- **A "time gap" on a CV** is necessarily not negative.

- **Headhunters** to be the very last option in the recruiting process.

Work Ethics. Never, ever, step outside the boundaries of proper work ethics. If ever doubting an eventual action, make a "reverse Nike", just don't do it!

Never hold back an associate's company career for the good of your own interests or for the good of your current hotel.

Loyalty. Nothing can replace loyalty towards your boss and colleagues.

The transition from GM to Area GM can be more challenging than anticipated.

For a slightly less stressful life as GM, make sure to always have a top-notch number two.

The way you leave is the way you will be remembered. Never to forget.

THE DARK SIDE

It was an eye-opening experience to join the dark side—a different and interesting side. The dark side can be defined as parts of a person, a group, an activity, etc. that are unpleasant, evil, or harmful. In this case, the dark side is the owner of the asset, the hotel, that a GM operates on behalf of a management company. Most often jokingly, however, it's far from uncommon to hear GMs complaining about their "owner rep on the dark side."

As a GM, you deal with owners and owner representatives on a regular basis. Today, a representative of the owner would most often have the title Asset Manager (AM), which is a far better "job description." To put it briefly, the role of an asset manager is to support the operations to optimize the performance, as well as to make sure that there is a proper upkeep of the hotel. Frequently the main objective is to increase the value of the hotel in preparation for a future sale.

During my close to five years as asset manager with Gaw Capital Partners Hospitality (GCPH), I dealt with some of the main international chains: Accor, Hyatt, Marriott, and InterContinental – "same, same but only marginal different." In my experience, the corporate backbone, being the loyalty program, S&M initiatives, reservation system or operational support does not differ much. When you are AM for a hotel operated by one of the big international chains, it's not only important to establish a good working relation with the GM, but also with the corporate office, usually an area office. To put it bluntly, you need to wake up the corporate area executives now and then, so they focus a bit extra on your hotel as they often have another 15-20 hotels to worry about. I am specifically referring to sales and marketing. However, one thing is for sure, the GM and team are the ones that will "make it or break it", not the corporate office, regardless of which management company is operating the hotel.

What is a good GM in the eyes of the asset manager, and what is a good asset manager in the eyes of the GM?

It's quite easy to describe a GM to the liking of the AM. It's the GM that will consistently deliver desired results and keep the asset, the hotel, in very good shape, regardless of the level of corporate support. A strong individual who keeps the AM up-to-date and who is always transparent in communication and behavior. A person who can be trusted. One should not forget that the AM might, for whatever reason, have a different view of the qualities of the GM than the GM's corporate boss. The GM can be "God's gift to the hotel industry" in the eyes of the executives of the operator, but if the GM is not in the good books with the owner/AM, the GM should contact the corporate HR department to discuss relocation. Under such circumstances it's not even worth the effort by the corporate office trying to keep the GM in the current hotel.

Many AMs are former hoteliers, working for a specialized hotel asset management company, or a person from the owning company "best suited" for the assignment, often with a real estate background. Regardless of background, the challenge for the AM is not to micromanage. Especially as a former hotel executive it takes time to get used to being on the sideline and not being involved in the daily operations. You have to trust the GM and team and let them do their job. In due course, normally monthly, there will be meetings to discuss the performance of the hotel, and to exchange ideas. Bear in mind that the AM also has "higher powers" to report to and needs to justify the financial results, which might not always be as predicted.

Time to stick out my neck – far too many asset managers focus exclusively on the figures. This is an easy way to "show strengths." The GM missed the monthly budget – baseball bat on the left knee. Makes the budget but misses the forecast – right knee. Makes budget and forecast, but 2nd in the compset – both knees. There is nothing more basic and simpler than chasing figures. At the end of the day, owners are most often in it for the money, hence the bottom line should obviously be a top priority. I am only saying that just as important, and to be taken into consideration, are what actions have been taken to fulfill the financial expectations, and how the strategy looks going forward. I know very capable and professional GM colleagues that have been forced to leave their hotel because of unprofessional AMs, usually the ones exclusively focusing on figures.

During my combined 25 years as Executive Assistant Manager, Resident Manager, General Manager and Area General Manager, I dealt with my fair share of owners/asset managers. Some have been more demanding than others and some have, at times, been too anxious to chase figures to justify their own existence as AM. As AM, I genuinely tried to support the GM, assisted by my background in operations, and I would rather pick up the mobile phone for discussions instead of sending strong emails. More than once I reviewed a drafted email to a GM and said to myself, "How would I, as GM, react if receiving this message?" I pressed the delete button when realizing that my message would only generate demotivation and bad vibes. My "AM school" was my experience as GM, being able to learn from the AMs that I dealt with. It's "the classic", treat people the way you want to be treated. It's more productive, and more enjoyable that way.

I used to say: "The life as a GM ends at the GOP line, and the life as an AM starts below the GOP line." This is not the full story, as the AM is involved in supporting the GM to achieve the GOP. It's to highlight that there are more important considerations for the owner below the GOP line. As mentioned earlier, if the financial obligations for the owner require better than budgeted GOP, let the operator know about it.

As most companies involved in asset management, at GCPH, we received a lot of information following the monthly closing. We tried to a large extent to keep to the reporting of the operating company, however there were a number of templates and reporting documents specially designed by us for the GMs and teams to complete. I once messed up big time in one hotel by not thoroughly reviewing the documents relating to accounts receivable. One wouldn't think this is a job for the AM, it should obviously be something to be controlled by the finance department of the hotel. However, my blunder was a good learning experience that unfortunately caused a write-off.

One advantage of working with the team of GCPH, was that we all had a vast experience from operations. Especially in Asia, the operators were very much aware of this fact. This had two main advantages in our relationship with the operators. Firstly, they all knew that we didn't accept anything but genuine facts and actions, no odd excuses or "beautifying." Second, they appreciated our feedback, and did gather their resources and acted relatively fast on our recommendations, even if not always as efficiently as desired.

The inspiring and hectic life as an asset manager was a perfect bridge from my previous, even more hectic life as area GM, thereafter, transiting to the non-hectic life as 2/3-retired. My life as an asset manager meant a lot of travel, normally three weeks out of four. More than a couple of days in the Bangkok office and I had "ants in my pants", hence the life on the road/tarmac suited me very well. I worked better in a boring airport lounge than in the office, despite having fantastic colleagues. From having south Thailand as an area with Anantara to constant travel to Vietnam, Myanmar, Singapore, Hong Kong, Japan, South Korea, and Australia meant a bit of adjustment, but as said, I truly enjoyed it.

Maybe the best part was when Chris Vielle, my boss and at the time CEO of GCPH, asked me to make a first assessment of a hotel; "Go to X and check out Y hotel, also have a look at the closest competitors". I enjoyed it the most when I was incognito and could move around as a regular guest. This was obviously just a "first scratch on the surface" to give an indication if it would be worthwhile to pursue more work for a future eventual acquisition.

If only in the due diligence process, it was a great

experience to be involved in the sale of the Hyatt Regency Osaka in 2016, two and a half years after the acquisition. This was a true example of an amazing financial turnaround, initiated, and masterminded, by the owner. To quote Chris Vielle: "When we bought the hotel, it was losing Y 300 million per year in NOI. This year the hotel will be making over Y 500 million in profit. We achieved this by improving both room rate and occupancy, streamlining operations and installing a power plant to improve energy efficiency, in combination with substantial growth in Japan tourism growth." (Pere News) Turnaround of close to US$ 6 million in 2 ½ years.

In addition to my normal duties at the InterConti Hotel in Hong Kong, as asset manager, I was for close to two years heavily engaged in the approximate US$ 250 million total renovation of the hotel. The US$ 738 million acquisition, in July 2015, of the 503 room hotel was successfully led by Gaw Capital Partners. IHG sold the hotel but stayed on with a long term management agreement. Supporting Chris Vielle in keeping all stakeholders informed, and supporting in coordination of input from architects, interior designers, project manager, various consultants, investors, and IHG was a fantastic learning experience, though causing a few sleepless nights. However, it was by far the most interesting, and challenging, part of my life as an asset manager. The hotel was re-opened in 2023, much delayed, amongst others due to the Covid pandemic. It was then branded as Regent Hong Kong, representing the top luxury brand of IHG.

Once again I will mention my favorite words: transparency and trust! If this is established between the two managers – Asset and General, at least the base for a smooth working relationship has been established. To a general manager, life as an asset manager sounds comfortable. Even though an asset manager is supporting in the way the operator generates the GOP, the focus can never leave the financial status below the GOP line. I can assure you that life can be more comfortable above the GOP line than below the same.

What I have learned

Key priorities for an asset manager:

- **Provide the GM with regular feedback**, however, stay away from micromanagement. Leave the GM and team to run the show.

- **Figures and bottom line** of utmost importance, but do not become purely a "figure chaser".

- **The upkeep of the hotel** to be in focus. Ensure there is a detailed preventive maintenance program in place and scrutinize Capex projects.

- **Agree on one (!) yearly budget** with the operator.

- **Make sure there is a well-outlined strategy** to support the budgeted figures.

- **Establish close working relationship** also with the corporate office of the operator.

- **Well in advance of a management agreement's expiring date,** ask yourself if the hotel could benefit from a different operating company.

Transparency will lead to trust. A good base for the working relationship between the asset manager and the general manager.

The ideal background of an asset manager is most often hotel operations.

The GM and team are the ones that will "make it or break it", not the corporate office, regardless of which management company is operating the hotel.

The dark side should never be underestimated by the operator.

UNFORGETTABLE MEMORIES

Let me portray a few unique episodes that I have encountered over the years.

How to tease a competitor

Kalvøyafestivalen was a Norwegian music festival arranged outside Oslo, quite close to the Sheraton Hotel, hence many of the artists stayed with us. This is back in 1986. The day before the start of the festival, I received a call from Mrs. Gullaksen, the wife of Bjorn Gullaksen, the area executive of the SAS Hotels in Norway. I hardly knew Bjorn and had never met his wife. I obviously became very curious. She explained that their son Jonas was a mega-fan of Mark Knopfler of Dire Straits and asked if there would be a possibility for Jonas to have his autograph. Bjorn was probably upset not to have the famous artists staying at the SAS hotels, and for him to call the Director of Sales at the Sheraton to ask for such a favor could maybe be too tough to swallow.

For breakfast the following morning, all members of Dire Straits signed their autographs with a nice message to Jonas. The good part is that they signed the cover of a bright yellow Sheraton weekend brochure. I immediately sent it, by express mail, to the home of the Gullaksen family. A few days later, a shy Jonas calls me and very politely thanks me for the gift. I couldn't resist, so I said to Jonas, "I think you should put up the brochure on the wall by your bed." Jonas agreed and I could visualize how Bjorn Gullaksen, every night when wishing his son good night, had to face a shining Sheraton logo over the bed. What a nightmare!

Reverse outcome

Due to unfortunate stranded negotiations between Sheraton Corporation and the owners of the Sheraton Hotel in Istanbul, the hotel was closed at the end of October 1994. As mentioned previously, the Director of Finance and I stayed on for the final handover to the owners. It was everything from issues with shop tenants to accounts receivable, not forgetting that Sheraton was very strong on the fact that we should not leave any trace of the Sheraton name or logo. No stationary, nothing.

The hotel is a 20-floor+ building next to Taksim Park with fantastic views over the Bosporus. This high rise was visible all over the city. The issue was that it was visible together with a mega Sheraton logo on top of the building. I must say that I was very pleased the day I left the hotel and found contractors working on dismantling the Sheraton crest from the building. A big, expensive undertaking. An important ingredient of the story is that, in those days, Istanbul was during wintertime heated with coal. Visualize a concrete-constructed building that has been exposed to very polluted air for a period of approximately 40 years. From light grey to light brown.

It was the first time I had arranged for this kind of work and my lack of experience nearly gave me a heart attack the following morning. The first thing I did after waking up was to look out of our bedroom window at the Hilton, that faced the Sheraton. I saw a bright mega Sheraton logo on the building. The dirty Sheraton crest had been removed and underneath was the original light grey colour, contrasting with the light brown of the rest of the building. Sheraton had never, ever, had such prominent exposure in Istanbul! Two days and many buckets of paint later and the logo was gone.

NEVER say NO to a guest

The process of opening the Sheraton Pine Cliffs in the Algarve, Portugal was long and frustrating. Finally, on the third (!) official opening date, we opened the doors in August 1992. It was the “crying wolf” scenario and when we finally opened, it took time to get business going. The limited number of guests we had from the start could really benefit from outstanding service, shame otherwise. The resort is located on the cliffs, overlooking Falesia Beach and the Atlantic Ocean, stunning.

One service still not up and running when we greeted our first guests was the elevator on the cliff edge, leading to the beach. There were stairs available, however some guests preferred our service to shuttle them with a Range Rover on a dirt track that ended about 500 meters away from our beach concession with sunbeds and towels. Our bell boys oversaw the SUV, and they had really adopted the motto: "NEVER SAY NO TO A GUEST". An American couple asked the bellboy to drive them on the beach from the end of the dirt track to the Sheraton concession. The answer was a prompt, "With pleasure"! The guests happily arrived at the beach beds, then the biggest vehicle mess in the history of Falesia Beach ensued. The Range Rover got stuck in the wet sand and slowly the tide was approaching. Desperation and a call to the fire brigade to pull the vehicle loose. They arrived too late, and the SUV drowned in the Atlantic Ocean.

The Range Rover was salvaged during the following low tide and the concept of "NEVER SAY NO TO A GUEST" had to be re-evaluated.

Locals know better

Amman is located 700 meters above sea level. However, I had never contemplated that we could have snow in Amman. How wrong I was. One February winter day, the forecast for the following morning was heavy snowfall. Several associates said that they needed to stay overnight in the hotel so they could take care of the breakfast service. Francois Waller, Resident Manager, and I, disagreed and sent everyone home.

Around 06.30 AM the following morning, I had Francois on the phone: "Look outside!" Two decimeters of snow, wind, and hail in the air. Even for a Swede, used to tough winter weather, this was on the rough side. No way to get the car on the roads.

Fast shower, "1/2 kg" of hair gel, got dressed and prepared for a brisk 20-to-30-minute walk to the hotel. Leaving the house, I was protected from the wind, until I came around the corner and the wind and hail hit me, big time. Hair gel, wind and hail, not the best combo. 45 seconds after leaving home, I was wearing an "ice helmet", talking about a brain freeze! This was the first, and one of the few times, we had snow in Amman. However, in more than one aspect—a good lesson learned.

Cultures facing each other

I have described Iraq as "the new Klondike" after the US invasion, and Amman as one of the key gateways to Bagdad. An illustration of those days once caught the attention of Helle. The sit-down check-in desks in the lobby each had two comfortable chairs, facing each other. In one chair sat the "classic American cowboy", dressed in jeans, boots, and a cowboy hat. He was facing a Middle Eastern man dressed in traditional Arabic clothing.

What a contrast facing each other, Amman was a true melting pot of people and cultures.

Frozen Oysters

In June of 2016, Banyan Tree was due to be introduced on the Singapore stock exchange. Prior to the IPO, finance gurus of Singapore were invited for a two-day visit to Laguna, Phuket. The instructions were clear, no effort or money was to be spared to impress this group of seven people.

Banyan Tree Hotel was to host the welcome dinner, and Sheraton the dinner the following evening. We closed our Thai restaurant for four days for decoration. The theme was "The Sky is the Limit," referring to the future of the Banyan Tree shares. The Chef and F&B Manager worked hard on the menu and wine selection. I was satisfied, it all looked fantastic.

Time for dinner, which also included the GMs of the six Laguna hotels. What came as a surprise was The Chef's "amuse bouche" to fit with the theme. We were presented with an oyster topped with Beluga caviar on dried ice, to visualize clouds in the sky. I have to say, not very smart to symbolize clouds when referring to the future of the Banyan Tree shares. Anyway, it looked very nice, and we were on to a great start to this important dinner. However, this was also the start of the most embarrassing experience in my hotel life.

If you ever come across oysters on dried ice, don't even consider trying it. The cold ice makes sure that the oyster gets stuck in its shell and when you finally succeed in dismantling the poor oyster, there is a great risk that it will get stuck in your palate.

Luckily, I had one lady in between me and KP, the chairman, which most probably saved me from getting a fork stuck in my leg. Instead, KP leaned behind the back of my female shield and softly said: "Jan, this didn't start too well." Then he loudly asked me to give a speech and tell the dinner guests everything about frozen oysters. Without a doubt, the low mark of any speech I have ever held, to the amusement and delight of some of my fellow GMs. I wonder if the Chef ever tried his own oyster invention.

Who are you?

When living in Copenhagen, and working for Ligula Hotels in south Sweden, the family took the 2012/ 2013 Christmas and New Year's break in Phuket. Very convenient as we still had our house there. Great for all of us to catch up with friends on the island. We lived in Laguna, close to the beach, and to me, more importantly, close to the golf course.

One day, arriving at the golf club, I ran into an old friend at the entrance, Bill O'Leary. Bill'O, "Mr. Amanpuri". Bill'O, in charge of boats and yachts and "I do not know what" for many years at Amanpuri, and therefore very familiar with the "Aman Junkies" (loyal Aman guests) around the globe. After a friendly hug, Billo says: "Let me introduce you to another hotelier, this is...... ". I didn't fully catch the name, only that it sounded familiar. As I am lousy with names and as lousy to recognize faces, I "shot from the hip": "How are you doing these days? I am shoveling snow in Copenhagen!" Then a good slap on his shoulder. I was answered in a relatively dry tone: "We own the Hyatts". A "light bulb moment", Tony of the Pritzker family, the owners of Hyatt Hotels Corporation.

I quickly disappeared into the restaurant, Bill'O

was not too impressed, and Tony Pritzker probably wondered, who the h... was that? Hoteliers – A big happy family!

More Champagne please

In December 2013, as GM of Anantara Riverside in Bangkok, I agreed with my Resident Manager, Markus Krebs, on how to allocate responsibilities during the upcoming Festive Season. I will take care of Christmas and Markus New Year's. Perfect, Helle and I will spend some relaxing days in Phuket over New Year's. To play safe, I made sure to inform my boss, the COO of Minor Hotels.

At the time I was Area GM of owned Anantara assets, including the upcoming Anantara Layan in Phuket. I was curious about the current state of the construction, and together with Helle, I drove to the site for a look (why bring your wife to a construction site?). Whilst on our tour, we bumped into Boyd Barker who was the interim GM from the corporate office. I got an update, and we quite soon thereafter left the site. A couple of minutes away, I get a call from Boyd:" Bill Heinecke would like to see the two of you for some refreshments on his yacht." The yacht was anchored close to the beach of the resort.

This is the kind of invitation that you do not even consider turning down, and why would you? A dinghy picked us up and soon we were onboard the yacht, together with Bill and Kathy Heinecke, their son John with wife and their two kids. A relaxing afternoon with the Heinecke family and Moët and Chandon, very nice.

Kathy asked me: "When did you arrive in Phuket?" I answered on Saturday (being December 28th). Silence, then Kathy said: "Jan, how long did you work for us?" This was her way of saying, how can you, as GM, be away from the Anantara Riverside over New Year? I got the point, but I didn't bother to explain about the duty set-up at Riverside. I remember that, after a bit of awkward silence, I politely asked for some more Champagne.

It was a great few hours on the yacht, also nice to see Bill Heinecke relaxing with the family. I didn't get one single question relating to business, except the one from his wife Kathy, which was said jokingly and with a twinkle in her eye, though a question never to be forgotten.

True Hospitality

First time in South Africa. Helle, Victor, not yet

two years old, and I arrived in Cape Town and were immediately exposed to a destination that understood hospitality. Families with children were guided to a special line at the passport control to make the arrival less stressful. Smiling staff and a great start to the vacation. And it became even better when arriving at our "hotel", Welgelegen Guesthouse, an old, beautifully maintained villa with a few tastefully decorated guest rooms. The kind of place that doesn't equip the rooms with a mini bar, instead you rob the kitchen fridge of a few beers and just scribble on a notepad on the kitchen table. The same table where you are served a great breakfast by the landlady. Despite all the fancy and extremely well-run hotels in the world, we couldn't have asked for more in terms of accommodation. We just loved this "homey" bed and breakfast atmosphere.

After a few days in and around Cape Town, guided by our driver Ike, it was time for Hermanus, a beautiful coastal area about a 90-minute drive from Cape Town, most famous for being the home of the Southern Right Whales spotting. No whales to be seen and after 24 hours, we were already longing back to Cape Town. The problem was that the whole city was fully booked, and not a hotel room was available. Ike came to our rescue. He was working on a freelance basis as a driver at the Holiday Inn.

Ike made a call to the GM of the hotel who gladly informed us that he just had a few no-shows. Even better, they were part of a pre-paid group, so Ike's friends, i.e. Victor and parents, were more than welcome to stay complimentary for the rest of their vacation in Cape Town. We had the great pleasure of meeting the GM upon our arrival at the hotel. It didn't take long before he invited us for a South African braii (BBQ) the same evening at his home in a suburb of Cape Town. Victor played in a small kids' pool, whilst Ike, Helle and I enjoyed an outstanding evening with the GM and his wife. Unforgettable True Hospitality!

What I have learned

Always expect the unexpected!

FAMILY

Tunisia, Egypt, Jordan, Thailand, Denmark – American school, British school, American school, British school, then International Baccalaureate. Take away destination Tunisia from our daughter Emilie and deduct Denmark from son Victor and you have a short description of the schooling of our third culture kids. Is this educational background, forced by their father's job as a hotelier, positive or negative? The alternative might have been schooling in Helle's home country Denmark, or Sweden, my home country.

During the US invasion of Iraq, in March 2003, there were, in some camps, negative sentiments towards the USA in Jordan. Except for key personnel at the embassy, US citizens were evacuated. Working for Starwood, an American company, and having the kids in the American school, we followed the recommendations of the US embassy, except that I stayed on in Amman.

Helle, Victor who was nine years old, and Emilie who was six and a half, left for Odense, Denmark, to stay with Helle's parents. Helle's father was the headmaster of a school, so he asked a colleague if the kids could attend the local school during the three months away from Jordan. This was great to improve their command of Danish. They could also experience the discipline, or lack thereof, in a Danish school and compare it to their normal environment in an international school. One thing is for sure, the discipline in the international schools is quite stringent, at least the ones that Victor and Emilie attended. As parents, a definite positive. Having English as their first language is another positive, this is on top of fluent Danish, thanks to Helle, and OK in Swedish and Spanish, the latter thanks to studies with exchange semesters in Spain.

Many youngsters go through four different schools; even though two different educational systems might not be too common, this "back and forth" was never an issue. A big difference is the IB, International Baccalaureate, compared to the high schools in Denmark or Sweden. There is a higher flexibility in the school systems in Scandinavia, enabling more choices of subjects, which makes a lot of sense. One can easily say that the IB studies are very tough, sometimes even too tough. One thing that is positive about IB is that students become very well prepared for future studies at the university level. Overall, the positives and negatives might even out, most importantly, the international school education has served Victor and Emilie well.

Schooling is one important factor in a youngster's life, but what about the social life? One big drawback is that they grow up without having any real "home base". Our kids lived in Phuket for the longest period of their youth. 6 ½ years with friends of many nationalities, now all spread around the world. If they go back to Phuket today, they will not find one single friend from their school days. Victor studied in Copenhagen, and is now working there, considering it his base, whilst Emilie is making London her base with work, after studies in Glasgow.

For Helle and I, it's been a question of keeping up contact with the families and friends in Sweden and Denmark. With summer vacations in Sweden, including visits to Denmark, we have had a good success rate. An obvious advantage has been my assignments in resorts; Hammamet (Tunisia), Soma Bay (Egypt), Phuket (Thailand), and Langkawi (Malaysia). You have more friends than ever when school holidays in Scandinavia are being planned. Sarcasm aside, it's been an incredible privilege to have had so many friends visiting us over the years. The record was set one Swedish winter school break, when friends, plus friends of friends, were occupying the beach of Soma Bay. Including kids, a total of 65 persons!

The expat life is impossible without a very supportive spouse, to say the least. Helle gave up a good job in Copenhagen to join my nomad life. Many mothers are driving their kids to school, but very few drive them through the Egyptian desert, a full-hour excursion to school, one-way, five days a week. To adapt to new destinations, and to be able to work, Helle, with a master's degree in economics, started as an assistant class teacher, before she earned a degree in teaching, to later top it up with a master's degree in education. She loves kids and books, hence her current life, working as a teacher librarian, is "hand in glove".

Living in Phuket, Helle singlehanded raised the kids for two years when I was working in Malaysia and Hong Kong. Then another one and a half years living in Copenhagen whilst I was based in Bangkok. At the time this set-up was unavoidable, though not desirable. I saw the family as often as possible, however, I still regularly think about it and wonder if there could have been a better solution.

Not only an extremely supporting wife, but also supporting kids. It has not always been a "walk in the park", though the two of them were fast adapting to new environments. Also Victor and Emilie deserve a lot of respect and admiration.

I have earlier touched on the importance of learning a new language in a new destination. It is as important for the children to pick up the language of their parents, should they not bring it along from home. In our case, Victor and Emillie studied Danish online with the support of Helle. In addition, we always spoke "Scandihovian" (Danish and Swedish, plus sometimes a beautiful mix) at home. I have, on many occasions, experienced "expat children" on vacation in Scandinavia, only being able to communicate in English—very frustrating situation for all concerned. The language studies entails a lot of extra effort, however, it's important and definitely worthwhile.

As a family, there is an interesting and positive side of relocations, which is bonding. The four of us each had challenges to tackle in new, and unknown, destinations. It was not that we started each morning by giving each other high fives, but we cared for each other to settle well, and together enjoy it.

The "fishbowl life," i.e., to have your "apartment," often re-configured hotel rooms, in the hotel where you are GM, might sound nice, but that is far from the reality. Convenient to take the elevator to work and have the possibility of meals delivered by room service; however not as pleasant to have every step monitored by associates of the hotel. I experienced this life in Istanbul, Soma Bay, Hong Kong, and Bangkok. Maybe the biggest downside is that it is impossible to fully relax from your duties as soon as you are within the premises of the hotel.

Sunday morning in Soma Bay, you are in a good mood, together with the family, on the way to the beach. Then a full ashtray in the corridor and a bit later, a guest loudly complaining that the room key doesn't work. You would rather still be in bed, instead of dealing with ashtrays and room keys, but you can simply not ignore it. A GM colleague of mine once commented on the life living in the hotel: "My wife is the best Resident Manager there is. She sees everything and reports it to me." Helle and I had a mutual understanding, no Resident Manager on her part. With such a defensive husband, it would have been fatal for the marriage.

One frustration of working for an international management company is the process of transfer from one hotel to the other. Normally, as per the management agreement, the owner has the right to approve the GM and would ask to interview two or three candidates. You put your name in the hat because you are really interested in the hotel and location. Checking online and seeking advice from peers about the hotel, competition, schools etc. Helle and I kept the kids out of this exciting, but frustrating process, not to create expectations and unnecessary anxiety. It's irritating enough for the parents not to get the move that you have been aiming for. Luckily, it only happened once.

It should also be said that you hardly turn down the first suggested appointment as GM because of the location. Maybe, this is an option when it's time for the second assignment. As of the third GM relocation, assuming you are "in the good books", you can start to be picky about the next destination.

For an aspiring future GM of an international hotel chain, maybe you should read this chapter one more time. It's not written to discourage, it's written to give a "quite normal" picture of the family life as an international hotelier—an astonishing life!

What I have learned

Support from your partner is everything. Make sure that both of you are committed to the demanding, but exciting, international family life before deciding on this path.

The first assignment as GM will not be in central London, Hong Kong, or New York. Prepare yourself and your partner for an eventual hardship destination. It could become a lonely life for a non-working partner.

Schooling. Avoid relocation during the crucial final years of the children's education.

Language. The children to hold on to, or sometimes even learn, the mother tongue of their parents.

Family is more than you, your spouse, and your kids. It's also your parents and parents-in-law, the kids' grandparents, to take into consideration, especially when they reach a senior age. Make sure to keep up close contact.

The extraordinary family life as a hotelier, to experience different environments, destinations and cultures is unbeatable.

CAREER PLANNING

Career planning was never in my thoughts. I joined the hotel industry because I was attracted to and curious about hotels, but I had no knowledge about life as a hotelier. My ultimate goal was to become a GM without having a clue how to achieve it. The recipe was to work hard and then see where the efforts would bring me. Maybe not what can be called career planning, or maybe, to some degree, it was. At least I had a foot in the business, and I had a long-term goal, sometimes that's enough as career planning.

For a hotel school student, or anyone aiming at becoming GM, I do not think you can plan further than to target the next desired position, and then work hard. There are too many non-controllable variables at play; the performance of the hotel, the relation to your boss and fellow associates, as well as timing and luck. It's much easier if you plan your career, for example, as a tennis player, to think that "by the end of next year, I should be ranked amongst the top 250 in the world, and I will achieve it by improving my second serve and backhand volley." A plan with a clear time frame, goal and means of how to reach it. It's not as easy for an aspiring hotelier. However, set a time frame for a short – or midterm goal, and if succeeding in achieving your target, probably a specific position, go for the next one. If you do not make it, ask yourself why and re-evaluate the goal and timing.

What often can be of valuable support is to have a mentor, a person who can support and guide you in your professional life. Ideally an experienced hotelier higher up in the hotel hierarchy. The person will not always have all the answers but can advise you towards the best direction and/or action to take, or not to take. It's comforting to have a more senior person to trust and lean towards during your career. If not a hotelier, a mentor can well be someone with more business – and life experience and, importantly, someone possessing common sense.

One piece of advice, stay away from internal politics, it usually backfires. A second piece of advice, maybe (?!) at the end of your career, there is a possibility to adopt the saying, "don't work hard, work smart," but do not start off with that in mind.

As in any business, to climb the ladder, you must work smart AND hard, there are no shortcuts.

Let's go back in time and look at the criteria to become a GM. Here we go again, 80/20. When I started in the hotel business, 80% of the GMs had a background in F&B and 20% in front office/rooms, not 100% accurate, but very close to reality. Today, it's a totally different scenario to become GM. As earlier highlighted, a GM has to master the jungle of sales and marketing (S&M). The complexity of S&M makes it a necessity to benefit from specialists, however, a GM must feel comfortable in this jungle and be able to contribute to the decision-making. Early in your career, make sure to gain experience in the fields of revenue management, ecommerce, and social media. During my time as an asset manager, I reviewed CVs for GM appointments on a couple of occasions. With few exceptions, the ones with exclusively F&B backgrounds ended up upside down in the bottom of the pile.

To join a hotel school is an obvious step in career planning, even though I understand that less than 50% of the students pursue a career as a hotelier. In any specialized education, it is natural to have a number of students jumping the ship. In addition, the service-minded attitude of a hotel school student is attractive to any industry with close customer relations.

Regardless of your background, regardless of where you want to pursue your hotel life, to me, joining one of the main international hotel chains is the best education you can wish for. It can be tempting to accept a more senior role with an independent hotel, which is great if that's your aim for the future. You have to keep in mind that it's very hard to join the "big ones" once you are established with an independent hotel. The other way around is much easier. Simply because the international chains have internally such a big number of capable associates, making it very hard for an outsider to join. This is the case in the entire hotel hierarchy, including the GM's level. On the other hand, the independent hotel knows that the international chain hotels have a lot to offer in terms of training, and most often, welcome a person with this background.

Do not be blinded by the position. Before you accept any new position, make sure that you feel comfortable with the boss, make sure it is the right chemistry. Once again, temptation can take overhand. The optimal position might be offered to you, but it could become anything but pleasant if you do not appreciate, and can deal with, the working environment and your new boss. If you hesitate, I suggest that you wait. Do not rush your career, more opportunities will pop up. For the hotel school student, your semesters as a trainee cannot be underestimated. Look at it as if it might be your future employer after examination. As earlier highlighted, the opening of a hotel is something unique and would be a fantastic post as a trainee.

Where to grow your career as a hotelier? There are many considerations that play a vital role. Maybe the most important one is how far away from your home base that you are willing to go. I have tried Europe, North Africa, the Middle East, and Asia. I will stay away from any recommendations. I can only say that, for me personally, the most satisfying working environment was in Thailand. Overall a superior service, but as important, a relatively low payroll with flexibility in engaging extra staffing based on needs. In Asia you can provide top service without killing your bottom line which is very gratifying as a hotelier. Shortly put, you are spoiled. Another point is that you are also relatively spoiled in terms of remuneration, at least compared to Europe.

What I have learned

Career planning is very difficult, sometimes impossible, as there are many non-controllables that will influence the future. Short – and midterm planning with a specific goal and time frame is feasible.

Experience of ecommerce, social media and revenue management is of great importance for the career.

From big to small is much easier than the other way around.

"**Choose your boss**". Do not become blinded by a potential new position. If you do not feel comfortable with the working environment, especially if you have doubts about the eventual new boss, stay away.

A mentor is many times very valuable.

Never be afraid of taking responsibility, even when you are outside your comfort zone and risk failing. No worries, your attitude will be recognized.

Consistently, work smart AND hard and a bright career will follow.

EPILOGUE

Friday, January 31, 2020, my last day as an employed hotelier.

January 30, 2020. I was in Danang, Vietnam, with Yves Subsol, CFO of GCPH. Yves was taking over my asset management responsibilities for the Hyatt Regency Danang, hence we had a couple of days of handover. Then came the first company email relating to special action plans as a consequence of the Covid pandemic. Timing, or rather pure luck, was on my side. I was reading the mail on my mobile, showed it to Yves, and said with a smile: "It's all yours! Don't forget my farewell lunch in Bangkok tomorrow."

A fantastic 4L (Late Long Liquid Lunch) on January 31st, five months of relaxation in Phuket, though disturbed by rigorous Covid restrictions, summer in Sweden and then off to live in the Netherlands where Helle started her new job at the International School of Amsterdam. Two advisory assignments, in Stockholm and Copenhagen, and a lot of free time to write a book.

A book with the aim to give a picture of life as an international hotelier. A picture of pros and cons/opportunities and challenges, though exclusively based on my personal experiences. A picture that they don't paint at hotel schools. A picture that might have discouraged a few, but hopefully encouraged many more to pursue the exciting life as a hotelier.

APPENDIX 1

MY JOURNEY (indicative timing)

- Sheraton Stockholm, Sweden, Sales Executive & Sales Manager, 1982 – 1984
- Sheraton Hotel Oslo Fjord & Sheraton Sales Centre, Oslo, Norway, Director of Sales, 1984 -1986
- Sheraton Gothenburg, Sweden, Director of Sales, 1986 – 1988
- Sheraton Limassol, Cyprus, Executive Assistant Manager, 1988 – 1990
- Sheraton Antalya, Turkey, Interim Resident Manager, 1990 (6 months)
- Sheraton Pine Cliffs - Luxury Collection, Algarve, Portugal, Resident Manager, 1990-1994
- Sheraton Istanbul, Turkey, Resident Manager, 1994 (10 months)

- Sheraton Munich, Germany, Interim Resident Manager, 1994 (1 month)
- Sheraton Hammamet, Tunisia, General Manager, 1995 – 1999
- Sheraton Soma Bay, Egypt, General Manager, 1999- 2002
- Sheraton Amman Al Nabil Hotel & Towers, Jordan, General Manager, 2002 – 2005
- Sheraton Grande Laguna Phuket - Luxury Collection, Thailand, General Manager, 2006 – 2009
- The Andaman – Luxury Collection, Langkawi, Malaysia, Interim General Manager, 2010 (6 months)
- W & Sheraton Hotel, Maldives, Interim Cluster General Manager, 2010 (1 month)
- Regal Airport Hotel, Hong Kong, General Manager & Project Director, 2011 – 2012
- Ligula Hotels, Helsingborg & Malmo, Sweden, Interim General Manager, 2012-2013 (8 months)

- Anantara Riverside Hotel, Bangkok, Thailand, General Manager & Area General Manager - Owned Anantara Assets (Minor Hotel Group), 2013-2014.
- Anantara Phuket Villas, Phuket, Thailand, General Manager & Area General Manager - South Thailand, Anantara Hotels (Minor Hotel Group), 2014 – 2015
- Gaw Capital Partners Hospitality (Gaw Capital Group), Bangkok, Thailand, VP Asset Management, 2015-2020
- Freelance Advisor, Amsterdam, The Netherlands, as of August 2020

APPENDIX 2

THE QUESTION with Answers

Give me 3 criteria for being successful as a GM. This is what I asked several GMs and corporate executives, current and retired, to provide me with. This was not an attempt to conduct a sophisticated survey, by any means, only to collect the thoughts from a few hoteliers, some more experienced than others, with combined working fields in Europe, Africa, the Middle East, Asia, and the USA. I also received input from hotel school students.

Following are the 15 answers received. In my email, I also wrote: “Please feel free to elaborate as much/little as you want,” which can be read from the answers. I have kept them as intact as possible. Not to disclose the identity of the author, some comments have been left out. It’s a lot of feedback to digest, but maybe the most interesting part of this book.

CEO

• Gather a great team around you and then empower them to be great.

• Maintain a velvet glove for dealing with people, but ensure they always understand there is an iron claw underneath.

• Cultivate a sense of humor!

CEO

• Empathy and compassion. I often think of my first GM. It was his empathy and ability to connect with all those under him that made me realize I wanted to be a GM one day. I would have done anything for that man.

• Drive and commit. I often think of the hardest-working GMs under me. They were driven and always available 24/7 for their team and guests.

• Intelligence. Let's face it, if you're not thinking intelligently about your challenges and opportunities and acting appropriately on those, you'll never gain market share on your competitors, which is what your owner is paying you to do.

Former GM and SVP

• Hire employees with a friendly, positive attitude.

• Treat your team with respect and be humble.

• Maintain a loving, positive attitude with your team and customers, providing them with the Wow effect.

Cluster GM and former Asset Manager

• Team Player: Form a strong and diverse management team, foster open communication and involvement in decision-making, and promote a work-hard-play-hard environment. Avoid micromanagement, allowing freedom within the framework for the leadership team. Make it clear they can always seek advice and opinions rather than being constantly monitored.

• Empathy and Social Competence: Treat everyone openly and respectfully, the same way I was treated or wanted to be treated when starting my hotel career. This includes daily greetings with a smile, using employees' names, and acknowledging good and hard work. Show that employees' work-life balance is important, and rules around planning days off, holidays, overtime, etc., need to be adhered to by both employees and management. Be a good ambassador for your hotel/brand/company to guests, customers, and the local community. Have your meals at the staff restaurant.

• Reliable and Open Communication: Walk the talk, do what you said you would do, and expect the same from others. Stand up for your ideas and decisions, even in front of senior management or owners. Conduct monthly All Team meetings to update on the past month, including easy-to-understand KPIs around financial, quality, employee, and competitive evolution.

Former GM and SVP

• Manage owner relationships. They will control your destiny more than the chain you work for, so be one step ahead. Treat the hotel as if you are the owner, and communicate effectively.

• Get results. Ultimately, that's what matters to the owner of the hotel/chain or brand you work for, across all your KPIs. Set tough goals and exceed them.

• Lead and develop people. People have choices in who they work for. To attract and retain good people, and build a great culture. People seek leaders who help them advance their careers and enrich their lives through work.

If you succeed in all three, you will exceed. If you are lacking or falling short, and it's sometimes out of your control but you are putting in the effort, you may still survive. However, if you are missing the mark in two or more, you will not, and likely, you will be asked to move somewhere else.

Former GM and Area VP

- Passion
- Emotional Intelligence
- Integrity
- Courage to lead, courage to fight for what is right
- Leading by example

GM

• True and honest leadership: Put the interest of the hotel and the people before your own. If the hotel is successful, the people are successful, and subsequently, you are successful. Forget your ego; do it all without propaganda. This also creates loyalty.

• Be forward-looking: Have sustainable strategies and policies in place, set midterm to long-term goals, have a vision, but don't lose sight of the short term. The immediate P&L is as important as the long-term P&L.

• Reduce admin: Spend time in the operation and on the floor. Know your guests, know your staff. Too much analysis leads to paralysis.

GM

• Experience comes from being in the action, understanding each individual and department, and interacting daily with the team and guests.

• Bring out the best in people: Develop new leaders and ensure a positive work environment where team members can shine, are motivated, and empowered to go above and beyond for guests.

• Juggle well: If you can manage the above effectively, the business will be successful, and owners will be happy.

GM

- *The Human Resource Factor:*

There are no HR classes at a hotel school. Ever wondered why? Because it is the most difficult aspect of any business/corporation. We are in the people's business, we get told daily. True, but which company has ever gotten their HR side 100% right? It makes me think of parenthood. There are no manuals on how to raise a kid; there are books you can read, but rarely will you find the right book for your child, as your child is unique, one of a kind. The human element in our business is exactly the same—each associate is an individual, with individual needs, ambitions, problems, etc. The importance of the human factor varies from country to country, hotel to hotel, business model to business model. In developed countries, a job is a job; it's there for the associate to earn a salary and live off it and easy to move on from. In developing countries, it is a way to survive, put a roof over your head, and put some food on the table. Then you have the Gulf states, where 90% of the associates are expatriates, living onsite, far away from their families, between 4 to 6 persons in one room, who, through their hardship, dedication, selfless acts, are able to provide for their entire families back home. Lately, in the Gulf, one manages expatriates (from rank and file to management) and Locals (the programs are called Saudization, Omanization, Emiratization, etc.) who have enjoyed decades of earning funds without having to work and now that they have to work only aspire/demand/accept the top jobs that they have no experience for. This then leads to internal struggles, rivalry, discrimination, and the list goes on.

It's in times of crisis that the human factor needs to stand out. Let's take the Covid-19 pandemic as a concrete example. When it started in March 2020, we all thought it was going to be a 3-month issue that would fade away. Keeping associates informed was still relatively easy as the message was well-defined by the company. Only very few discomforts and restrictive measures were put in place, but these were directly related to the health and safety of the associates. As the restrictions and timeline of the pandemic kept increasing, financial restrictions, hardship measures, etc., were harder to explain but ultimately understood. Job perpetuity was the key factor. What you are not prepared for is when associates lose family members and cannot travel. Many associates lost family members due to Covid, and having to comfort them, knowing very well that there is nothing one can do, is by far the hardest thing one has to deal with.

When looking at the most successful GMs, they all seem to have mastered the Human Factor. They get it right nearly all the time, or so at least it seems from the outside.

- *Owner Relations:*

Nothing at the Hotel school prepares you for owner relations. One gets taught how to run a hotel (somehow) but not of the importance of the owner. Owners vary from individual owners to families, to rulers of countries, to rich businessmen, to banks, investment funds, etc. Each of them has invested in the industry for different reasons. Some for prestige, some for pure financial results, some for a real estate deal, some out of tradition, some to show off, some as they did not know anything better to do with their money. Furthermore, owners are no longer linked to one brand/operator only. They compare, they negotiate, they know the business, they know the numbers, they know how to obtain special requests from the operating company. In short, they have mastered the way hotels operate, get sold, and most of all, can make profits. As a GM, we are expected to navigate this tightrope and hope that we have quickly mastered the art of recognizing what type of owner one deals with. Even though I have been a GM for nearly ... years, I still find this to be one of the most difficult aspects of being a GM.

When looking at the most successful GMs, they all seem to have mastered the art of owner relations.

- *Company Politics and Self-Promotion:*

Some GMs are very successful when it comes to running a hotel but are not very good at letting people know about it. They believe that the numbers/ results/statistics, etc., speak for themselves and that these are enough to be recognized. With hindsight today, I realize that I am one of those GMs who get the job done brilliantly in very hard destinations, old hotels with crappy owner situations without making noise about it. When we started over ... years ago in the industry, hard work, results, and your boss had to notice you to get on. Today, at the hotel school, one is not taught how to navigate the political aspects of large corporations.

In my opinion, the most remarkable GMs are the ones to have mastered the art of self-promotion and self-preservation.

There are many other aspects of our business that are not taught at hotel schools that one learns as one goes along. What to do in the case of financial crises, natural disasters, terrorism attacks, political unrest, wars, customer needs and requests, etc.

GM

• Know when to shut up and listen: This skill is crucial in various situations, including guest interactions and team discussions.

• Stay humble: Remember that you own nothing, and your success depends on hotel owners, their representatives, and your hotel management companies.

• Be able to communicate effectively: Deliver speeches and justifications for business results convincingly and know when to be blunt and honest.

Area GM

• Humility

• Integrity

• Passion

GM

• Build a great team you can trust.

• Never stop trying and learning.

• Stay curious, innovative, and don't fall into the comfort zone; break out of the framework and be bold.

Group Director

• Don’t micromanage; empower the team but always have your finger on the pulse.

• Listen to feedback and make decisions collectively with the team, but remember, it's not a democracy, and the buck stops with you.

• Understand finance and know how to analyze financial reports.

• Have a sense of humor!

Hotel School Student

• Be flexible both socially and professionally to achieve synergy among various departments.

• Be culturally talented to understand and cope with different cultures and personalities.

• Have a passion for attention to detail and scenario thinking to proactively prevent or enable events to reach perfection.

Hotel School Student

• Empathy: GMs in hotels must have a good level of empathy for guests and staff members to create a unique experience and ensure a well-functioning hotel.

• Stay true to yourself: Clearly communicate guidelines to guests to maintain the overall environment and values of the hotel.

• Be open to changes: Embrace new technology and trends while balancing proven ideas, allowing input from different people on various hierarchical levels.

Works Cited

BBC News. "Jordan 'not Afraid' after Bombs." BBC News, 10 Nov. 2005, news.bbc.co.uk/1/hi/world/middle_east/4426458.stm. Accessed 21 Jan. 2024.

Carlzon, Jan. Moments of Truth. New York City, HarperCollinsPublishers, 1985.

"Corruption Perceptions Index." Transparency International, www.transparency.org/en/cpi/2022. Accessed 22 Jan. 2024.

Datai Hotel. "Snakes." The Datai, www.thedatai.com/experiences/nature/the-datai-diaries/snakes/. Accessed 21 Jan. 2024.

Gibbons, Serenity. "You and Your Business Have 7 Seconds to Make a First Impression: Here's How to Succeed." Forbes, 19 June 2018, www.forbes.com/sites/serenitygibbons/2018/06/19/you-have-7-seconds-to-make-a-first-impression-heres-how-to-succeed/?sh=108c5b256c20. Accessed 22 Jan. 2024.

Hines, Morgan, and Derek Catron. "Record Online Direct Bookings Are Driving Innovation in Hospitality, Survey Finds." PhocusWire, 11 Jan.

2024, www.phocuswire.com/h2c-study-hotel-online-bookings-digitalization. Accessed 22 Jan. 2024.

"Maya Angelou Quotes: 15 of the Best." The Guardian, 29 Apr. 2014, www.theguardian.com/books/2014/may/28/maya-angelou-in-fifteen-quotes. Accessed 22 Jan. 2024.

Nandi, Kathakali. "TikTok Influencing American's Tourism Discovery, Shows Survey." Hotels Magazine, 10 Apr. 2023, hotelsmag.com/news/tiktok-influencing-americans-tourism-discovery-shows-survey/. Accessed 22 Jan. 2024.

Nyst, Annabelle. "134 Social Media Statistics You Need to Know for 2023." Search Engine Journal, 14 July 2023,

www.searchenginejournal.com/social-media-statistics/480507/#:~:text=Social%20Media%20Statistics%20Worldwide&text=There%20are%204.8%20billion%20social,increase%20year%2Dover%2Dyear. Accessed 22 Jan. 2024.

PERE. "Gaw Sells Osaka Luxury Hotel for $153m." PERE, 3 Nov. 2016, www.perenews.com/gaw-sells-osaka-luxury-hotel-for-153m/. Accessed 22 Jan. 2024.

Rogers, Greg. "Saving Face and Losing Face." Tripsavvy, 26 Feb. 2020, www.tripsavvy.com/saving-face-and-losing-face-1458303. Accessed 22 Jan. 2024.

Stefan, Dana. "Tripadvisor Transparency Report Reveals 4.4% of Reviews Are Fake." Travel Tomorrow, 17 Apr. 2023, traveltomorrow.com/tripadvisor-transparency-report-reveals-4-4-of-reviews-are-fake/. Accessed 22 Jan. 2024.

UP Hotel Agency. "The Power of Social Media in the Hotel and Hospitality Industry." LinkedIn, 18 Apr. 2023, www.linkedin.com/pulse/power-social-media-hotel-hospitality-industry-up-hotel-agency/. Accessed 22 Jan. 2024.

"What Is Corruption?" Transparency International, www.transparency.org/en/what-is-corruption. Accessed 22 Jan. 2024.

"What Is the Difference between a Leader and a Manager?" Robert Half Talent Solutions, www.roberthalf.jp/en/management-advice/leadership/leader#:~:text=Overall%2C%20the%20key%20difference%20is,working%20towards%20the%20bigger%20picture. Accessed 22 Jan. 2024.

ACKNOWLEDGEMENTS

It is impossible to highlight anyone specific amongst the thousands of colleagues in all places, at all levels, that have transformed my life as a hotelier into an extraordinary experience.

Special thanks to former colleagues, hotelier friends and students who have contributed to this book with input relating to what makes a successful General Manager. Thanks to friends who have taken their valuable time to review the manuscript or parts of it.

I express my gratitude to Helle for her proofreading and appreciate the invaluable support of her, Victor and Emilie throughout the years "on the road," without which the journey would not have been as gratifying, enjoyable, and memorable – THANK YOU!